5 STEPS TO STORYTELLING POWER

JANIKA GALLOWAY

5 STEPS TO STORYTELLING POWER

HARNESS YOUR NARRATIVES AND TAKE CHARGE OF YOUR LIFE

Copyright © Janika Galloway 2023
First published by the kind press, 2023

The moral right of the author to be identified as the author of this work has been asserted.

All rights reserved. Without limiting the rights under copyright reserved above, no part of this publication may be reproduced, stored in or introduced into a retrieval system, or transmitted, in any form or by any means (electronic, mechanical, photocopying, recording or otherwise) without the prior written permission of the publisher of this book.

A catalogue record for this book is available from the National Library of Australia.

Trade Paperback ISBN: 978-0-6455978-5-1
eBook ISBN: 978-0-6458656-0-8

Cover design: Christa Moffitt, Christabella Designs
Author images: B Photography

Print information available on the last page.

The kind press acknowledges Australia's First Nations peoples as the traditional owners and custodians of this country, and we pay our respects to their elders, past and present.

THE
KIND
PRESS

www.thekindpress.com

We advise that the information contained in this book does not negate personal responsibility on the part of the reader for their own health and safety. The intent of the author is only to offer informative material on the subjects addressed in the publication to help you in your quest for emotional, physical, and spiritual well-being. While the publisher and author have used their best efforts in preparing this book, the material in this book is of the nature of general comment only. It is sold with the understanding that the author and publisher are not engaged in rendering advice or any other kind of personal or professional service in the book. In the event that you use any of the information in this book for yourself, the author and the publisher assume no responsibility for your actions.

To Ben,

Our two souls continue to weave their narratives in this lifetime.
This one, a love story that transcends the boundaries of space and time.

O & E,

Thank you for gifting me the precious story of motherhood.
A treasure that enriches my existence beyond measure.

CONTENTS

INTRODUCTION
Storytelling is in your DNA	iii
You are surrounded by stories and storytellers	iv
How I became a storytelling guide	vii

CHAPTER ONE
I'm a storyteller, nice to meet you — 1

You're a storyteller, too	4
Storytelling put simply	7
Losing your voice	8
The science of stories	10

CHAPTER TWO
You are the main character — 17

The greatest story of all	19
The body keeps the score	21
How our narratives hold us back	24
Uncover the stories worth sharing	28
What happens when we share?	30
The power is within you	32

CHAPTER THREE
Step 1: Making space for your narratives   35

The narrative of now   37
Which part are you playing?   43
Where you put your energy matters   45
Challenge your old stories   46
Uncover the gems in your timeline   49
Your experiences are what give you authority   54
Applying step 1 in real life   56

CHAPTER FOUR
Step 2: Knowing who you (truly) are   65

The role of the 'true self' in story   68
Reconnect with the passions of your inner child   73
A make-up bag for the soul   75
Applying step 2 in real life   83

CHAPTER FIVE
Step 3: Crafting a strong purpose   93

Getting anchored in your 'priority purpose'   96
What's holding you back?   99
Linking intentions to your purpose   103
Applying step 3 in real life   107

CHAPTER SIX
Step 4: Expressing yourself effectively   115

What's your communication flava?   118
Bonus communication channel: Tuning into the vibe   126

The art of expressing yourself	131
Assessing your audience	134
Applying step 4 in real life	138

CHAPTER SEVEN
Step 5: Conquering the storytelling pitfalls — 147

Pitfall 1: The self-sabotaging ego	150
Pitfall 2: Comparing your story with someone else's	156
Pitfall 3: Feeling like an impostor in your own narrative	159
Pitfall 4: Allowing your voice to be silenced	162
Applying step 5 in real life	166

CHAPTER EIGHT
Start sharing your stories — 177

Progress, not perfection	183
Become a force in the world	186
Your words are more powerful than you might think	188
The life-altering impact of stories	190
You've got the force	192

Notes	196
Acknowledgements	197
About the Author	199

INTRODUCTION

I was nine when I had my first encounter with the power of being a storyteller. I was an only child, and a furry puppy seemed just the buddy I needed. I'd spent six months (an eternity at that age) begging, pleading and nagging my parents to buy me a dog. The response was always a solid, 'No!', and always in unison. To make matters worse, when leaving the house they'd occasionally say, 'We're off to see a man about a dog.' I'd take that phrase literally, and my little heart would break when they'd return with no dog. Devastating.

I've tried asking nicely, I thought, *and they keep saying no. It's time to play with fire.* (Not literally! Geez, I wasn't that kind of kid.) I opted to tell them a story they couldn't refuse. I worked all week on my presentation and gave it everything I had, heart, soul and all. I pulled together every piece of craft available in the house and created a colourful poster detailing my points. The artwork even had pictures and drawings of adorable breeds that could work well within our family. I was going all out because I felt in my bones that this was my one remaining shot at pleading my case.

Finally, after dinner one evening, when both my parents were relaxing in the pitch-able zone of the oversized brown couch, I decided it was go-time. As I stood in front of them, heart thumping in my chest, it was clear as day that my future status as a pet owner hinged on my ability to deliver this story. Afterwards, a choice would be made that would impact my life in either a positive or negative way. The decision-making power sat with my parents, but I was acutely aware that the power of my story rested with me.

I'd rehearsed it all in front of my stuffed animals and dolls, holding onto my palm cards and pointing to the poster at just the right moments. And while the toys hadn't laughed at my jokes, I knew they'd appreciated my cute dress – it was Mum's favourite, too. I (thought I) knew my parents like the back of my hand – their motivations, frustrations, emotional soft spots and expectations – and I'd tailored my story to have maximum impact. I stood in front of them, ready to roll. Confident that tonight their 'no' would become a 'yes'.

When I finally spoke in front of them, poster, pink dress and all, they were so impressed with my effort to present that it intrigued them. They listened to me speak at length about this topic for the first time, and they actually heard me when I talked about being a lonely kid who was desperate for a playmate at home. I succeeded in connecting them with my emotional desire for a dog *and* my willingness to pick up its poo.

I was able to make them see how much owning a dog would mean to me. After I spoke, they could see that I wasn't just a nine-year-old nagging them to get her own way. I was a little girl who wanted another family member to love. When they said yes, a light turned on in my developing brain, and I collected an important life lesson: *Hmm. I can control an outcome if I tell a really good story.* That light continues to brighten my life today, and I know it can do the same for you.

Storytelling is in your DNA

Why did you pick up this book? Are you curious to learn more about storytelling as a concept? Or, did you see the word storyteller and identify with it? If so, that puts you a step ahead of most people, because the majority of people do not identify as being a storyteller, even though that's exactly what our species has been doing for thousands of years.

The walls of the Chauvet Cave in France are covered with what are considered to be some of the oldest known cave paintings in the world. These prehistoric drawings date back over 30,000 years, and tell the story of those early humans and the animals they hunted.

In Egypt, the paintings and hieroglyphics on the walls of some of the world's most mystical buildings tell the stories of great pharaohs, queens and gods. Hieroglyphics are one of the oldest forms of writing that exist, but to most Egyptians of that time, their meaning would have been indecipherable – written and understood by only the most educated members of society (usually the richest).

This was true of writing for most of our history, which is why the myths, legends and stories for the masses were either told visually – through art or performance, including my favourite mediums of dance, song and theatre – or orally, passed down through generations. Eventually, stories were collected and inked onto paper, allowing them to be preserved in books. With the birth of technology came other storytelling mediums: photography, radio, phones, television, movies and records. The digital age spawned other mediums of storytelling from blogs and videos to podcasts and social media.

Our modern storytelling landscape has seen the most significant shift of all because the internet has also lessened the power of the gatekeepers. Now, anyone with a wi-fi connection can access their desired medium and express themselves. It's no longer the privilege of the rich, educated or elite to decide who gets to share their stories. In many cases, storytellers can even choose who gets to consume their content – game-changing for storytellers like you and me! Not all storytelling mediums will suit the story you want to share, so finding the right medium for the story you're expressing is key. Who knows, drawings on caves might even be your thing!

You are surrounded by stories and storytellers

It's impossible to go through life without witnessing the power of storytelling in action. It surrounds and is woven into the fabric of everything from political campaigns, news stories, court trials and text messages, to advertisements, scientific research, social media posts, films, and events. The brands we interact with daily are all trying to sell us a certain 'story'. In fact, you're slicing story into your everyday life, too! If you get pulled over by a cop, what makes the difference between getting a ticket or not? A story. 'Sorry officer, I didn't even realise I was speeding. I'm rushing to the hospital because my wife is in labour right now'. Late for a meeting? Cue a story: 'Oh my goodness, you'll never believe the chaos on the way in this morning!'. Need a favour? 'Remember that time I helped you move house last summer? Well, my lease is up next month, and I could really use a hand with shifting the boxes'. When used effectively, storytelling is a useful skill that helps us connect and engage with, or influence others, yet many of us struggle to see ourselves as a storyteller, let alone open our toolbox (or voice box) to unlock its power.

I'm going to go out on a limb here and guess that when you think of a 'storyteller', an array of iconic speechmakers, authors, movie scenes or songs come to your mind's eye. Perhaps you picture a single person on a stage – against a black and red backdrop a la one of those TED Talks. Whatever and whomever you imagine, it's likely the person you picture seems confident, prepared, and proud. You might see 'storytellers' as people who've been granted the authority by society to be listened to and have been blessed with the confidence to express themselves.

Sure, the art of storytelling amplifies a voice and a message when correctly executed, but 'storyteller' is not a title you need to be given before you can access or utilise your story. You, my friend, are already a storyteller! We all have a story and some way of sharing it because every one of us is a living, breathing story. We're all writing our next chapter in this very moment because we are sourcing inspiration from and directing a narrative every single day in the book that is our life. Once we accept that we are the drivers of our story, we find we don't require approval from others to share it. It is simply ours to claim.

So many people I meet are unaware that they contain a multitude of stories. They are asleep to the narratives inside them, yet every heartbreak, lesson learned, success, failure, stroke of luck or moment of devastation has contributed to who they are and the lens through which they express themselves.

When we share a story, we share a piece of ourselves and allow others to peek behind the door that decodes our history, sheds light on our heart and reveals our intentions. This, in turn, allows for connection on a deeper level. Stories are how we express our humanity, and if you can tell yours in the right way and in the right moment, it has the power to move your life in the direction you desire. You might get a job over the many others who apply, be invited to the next party or land a second date with that person who gets your heart racing. Conversely, fail to express yourself and translate your life experiences in a way that resonates, and you might miss out on these dynamic shifts. In both scenarios, your stories are the same; it's your ability to harness them and then deliver them in a way that resonates that makes all the difference. No wonder people see the value of investing time and energy into being the best storyteller they can be.

Stories illuminate the truth of who we are and showcase hidden gems of wisdom. When examined, they can also reveal where we want to go next. Have you ever reflected on a chapter of your life and thought, *That experience/person/moment really mattered to me.* Or perhaps, *Nope! I sure as hell won't be making that mistake again.* The learnings that filter through from our experiences provide profound insights, which imbue our future storytelling with truth and authenticity, building an identity that sets us apart.

Even though we are born with an innate capacity to tap into the magic of storytelling, somewhere along the way in our transition from childhood to young adulthood, many of us lose our voices, or lose touch with the value of our stories and the importance they play in our life. Feelings of fear and unworthiness can creep in, making it harder to express ourselves and our desires, so we bury them in a sea of people-pleasing behaviour and conformity that keeps us small and silent. Pretty soon, this reduces us to playing a role in a story we're no longer the author of.

When you aren't writing your own story, you're likely to get swept up in narratives that are not designed for you. Eventually, you may struggle to recognise the person you've become. Reclaiming your human gift for storytelling is essential if you want to access the determination, resilience and creativity needed to propel you towards your dreams. Our true desires can be realised if we align with the story that lives within us and find the courage to express it, in whichever way we choose. Learning this lesson was transformative for me, which is why I've dedicated my life to storytelling – honouring its power while teaching others how to do the same.

How I became a storytelling guide

Incredible opportunities in my life have resulted simply from me sharing an inspiring or vulnerable story with the right person or confronting a story within myself. Of course, I've also had some horrendous experiences, but most of the time those revealed lessons so important and vital to my life that I can't imagine a path without them – no matter how devastating or difficult they were at the time. The good and the bad are equally as important in the book that is *Janika*, and to the concept that is storytelling power.

I've been on a mission to awaken individuals to the significance of their personal narratives within the context of their life. I guide them towards embracing their role as the master storyteller of their own lives irrespective of their background, status or past experiences. I teach clients that by connecting with their inner strength, they gain wisdom, and a profound knowledge of how the power of telling their story (even if only to themselves) can truly transform their existence. Through my work, which blends multiple types of storytelling (sessions, workshops, podcasts, writing, etc.), clients learn that the inherent force to own their stories, write their narrative and shape their destiny already lies within them.

The people I work with are wonderfully diverse, which is a testament to how storytelling touches us in every stage of life or profession. I've guided those who are entrepreneurial in nature, those who work with energy healing, and those with their own psychology clinics. Most have come to me to answer a similar calling: they have an overwhelming desire to step into their true story, want to follow or share their truth, and they want a solid roadmap to follow while learning to do this. We often start this work by exploring what their true story is, or by examining one specific story, as I usually find the underlying narrative of that story will intertwine with multiple chapters of their life.

Lucy (not her real name) is a great example of this. She came to me feeling flat, uninspired and tapped out of energy. Initially, we explored the narrative surrounding her work life. She was a nurse feeling exhausted after the global pandemic, and it's not hard to understand why. However, as we dived deeper, Lucy revealed that while she enjoyed helping people, she'd always felt the weight of carrying other people's problems on her shoulders.

It seemed Lucy had fallen into a pattern of being her family's emotional caretaker long ago and was always the first person to be dumped on when one of them had a problem. After decades of being told she'd be a great nurse because she was so caring, she had fallen into that career. The more we reviewed her narratives, the more we saw that this caretaking was a pattern. She'd use most of her energy helping others, only to leave her own needs ignored and her energy depleted. As a result, she spent a lot of her life feeling flat.

We worked on connecting Lucy back to her authority as the storyteller in her own life. By tapping into this power, she realised she required more balance and that to achieve this, she'd have to put boundaries in place in both her work and personal life. Lucy reclaimed her life story by moving to a new job with no weekend work for a better work–life balance. She also implemented a no weekend call rule for her family (unless for emergencies).

In my work I've seen people leave jobs that did not satisfy them, develop the courage to ask their crush on a date, or finally admit to themselves that they haven't been living their true story and actively make a change. This ability to shift in such a way and call on our inner strength so we can start living in and sharing our truth makes us a powerful force in the world because when we express ourselves from this place, our story feels most solid. I swear, this transformation is visible! Suddenly, a person seems more confident, stable and expressive. People around them start thinking, *Hang on, what happened to her? She seems on top of the world.* I call it the 'what are they on?' effect. The truth is, they are high on their own life story and claiming it as their own.

This book exists because of the course I created for clients to help them reconnect to their storytelling power and realise the gifts that can bring. Now, I've refined and expanded that course to help you do the same. *Great, you might be thinking, another self-help book that wants to point out all the mistakes I've made and the shitty stories in my life are all my fault. And, oh! While we're at it, let's add another role to my growing list of responsibilities: parent, spouse, friend, employee, business owner AND now 'storyteller'.*

Wait! Please don't close this book. I promise you, that ain't it! My goal is to show you how you can take those 'shitty stories' and use them along with every facet of who you are (positive and negative) to benefit your life. Your mistakes and experiences are the source of your wisdom; they're what give you the authority to share your story as only you can. I'm simply here to remind you how powerful you can be when you do that.

The storytelling power that I help people tap into is a grounded approach to narrative expression that makes you a more confident, direct, and compelling storyteller. I've developed five steps to help people harness this power based on the personal and professional learnings I've acquired in over a decade working as a storyteller and now guide. Each of these steps will make you a more powerful storyteller.

Anyone, regardless of their circumstance or status, can use them to express themselves more authentically and take control of their own narratives. You need not wait to be told you are worthy of being heard or worthy of writing your own narrative. As you'll soon find out, the power is already within you, in all its unique glory.

The 5 steps to storytelling power

Each one of the five steps that follow include real-life strategies that you can use to make a difference in your everyday life. I didn't want to write another storytelling book that bored you to death with big ideas and unrealistic promises. I want to showcase that we, as ordinary people, can execute expressions of who we are and share that to benefit our existence. When you place your story on a solid foundation, feeling secure in your inner connection, you can communicate with power.

Use these steps as a practical guide to standing true in who you are and what you want to express no matter which situation you find yourself in. Chapters 3 to 7 are each dedicated to one of the steps, and within each of those chapters you'll find a breakdown of the key concept followed by ways to apply that step to three key areas of life: work, relationships and your relationship with yourself. I told you, I'm all about giving you information you use in your real life, there are no impractical concepts here! Implementing these five steps will help you take charge of your life, but I encourage you not to skip a chapter. Even if you feel you're solid in a particular concept or familiar with a certain idea, please stay open to the idea of gaining further insights and work through the steps in order.

5 STEPS TO STORYTELLING POWER

Step 1: Making space for your narratives

First, we'll explore the timeline of your life and the narrative you're living right now. We'll take time to evaluate your level of awareness when it comes to how you've been conditioned, which beliefs you hold and where they come from. The stories you've told and roles you've played will reveal the person you've been up until this point. Once you are clear about that, you'll have the opportunity to question whether that version of you is true, or if it's time to recalibrate. Together, we'll integrate your past, present and future narratives so you can build a solid foundation for the stories you want to write in the future.

Step 2: Knowing who you (truly) are

Next, we will work on reclaiming your sense of self and initiating a homecoming to who you really are. By the end of this step, you'll be able to answer big questions, like 'Who am I?'. You'll understand how standing in your truth and living in alignment with your values, passions and beliefs, gives you the power to express these aspects of yourself more fully.

Step 3: Crafting a strong purpose

Once you know who you are and what matters to you, I'll show you how to create intentions for your future narratives that are anchored in your sense of purpose and sense of self. When your stories originate from this place, you build confidence in their value and your ability to use them to your advantage.

Step 4: Expressing yourself effectively

Your method of expressing yourself will shift and evolve as you gain insight into the art of expressing yourself. In this step, you'll learn to tailor your messaging to the form and style of communication that works best for you so you can land your story every time.

Step 5: Conquering the storytelling pitfalls

Finally, we'll talk about conquering the storytelling pitfalls and will explore tools to combat imposter syndrome, story silencing, dealing with the ego and more. You'll finish off strong and be ready to engage in expression.

After reading this book, I know you'll want to put these learnings into action and test their methods right away. And that's great, because that's the whole reason I'm sharing them! Bring them into your life and use the practical strategies and principles to express yourself more authentically and take charge of your life by directing the most important narrative of all: your own.

CHAPTER ONE

I'm a storyteller, nice to meet you

At school, my favourite subjects were drama, English and dance, and I enjoyed dance so much I even chose it for my main elective throughout high school. I'm not sure why I thought this was a good idea. Compared to my peers I was a terrible dancer – my limbs went in all the wrong directions on all the wrong counts, and to make matters worse my classmates had also given me the mortifying nickname of 'Pancake Ass' thanks to my lanky frame.

As much as I tried hiding my body in the back row, I stood out from other girls my age. I was taller by several inches, not to mention one of the only people with coloured skin in a very white city. While it wasn't fun being teased by my peers for standing out, it ended up leading to a modelling career after a local agent scouted me at a Brisbane shopping mall while out with my mum. She insisted that being taller and looking different to other girls was actually a good thing, and that I ought to try this catwalk thing out. So, from the ages of 14 to 20, my pancake ass and I travelled the world, getting paid to model in fashion weeks and help clothes, cities and brands tell their stories. I adored my Australian agency who had nurtured me, and with everything going so well, I was advised to move to Los Angeles and seize the opportunities coming my way. So, I did.

My modelling career came to a screeching halt when, at 20, I transitioned from 'girl' to 'woman' with wider hips than the industry desired. This, combined with the fact that I was consistently cast as the token 'ethnic girl', meant I just wasn't cutting it. No matter how good a model I was, this was an era of most clients wanting to tell stories that were 'whitewashed', so there were few places for me. Being the token made it very difficult to earn a living, and my heart was screaming for more.

It's strange when you live a 'dream' you thought would make you happy only to realise years later that those dream days were some of the most challenging chapters in your story. During my modelling years abroad, everyone told me how lucky I was to have the opportunity to meet popular photographers, wear designer clothes and travel the world. You'd think I was happy to be rubbing shoulders with famous people like Matthew McConaughey on set, or partying at Seth MacFarlane's house in the hills. But in reality, these were some of the lowest points of my life because I felt so far away from everything and everyone that was real and important to me.

I made some of the worst choices of my life during these years and I have no doubt this is because I stepped into stories that didn't align with who I truly was. Modelling agents consistently placed me in uncomfortable situations where I was fed unhealthy narratives about what I should value: men with money, having the smallest body I could possibly achieve and being agreeable at all times.

Slowly, the vultures exploiting my innocence and deep sense of disconnection swallowed me whole in the city of angels. (Dark, huh?) I wound up lost and lonely in body, and spirit. Spending all my energy trying to be the version of myself casting agents wanted had left me a voiceless chameleon.

This took a toll on me because we're not made to be still and silent. We're made to own our voices and champion them in whichever way we best express ourselves, and when we don't, we lose our power. One night, after doing something completely out of character for me, I looked in the mirror and didn't recognise myself. I didn't feel connected to this version of Janika, or the story she was crafting for our life. I decided it was time to move home to Australia and get to know myself again. I would reclaim my voice, and get an education while I was at it.

I'd dropped out of university a few years before this, but this time, I enrolled in a communications degree and was determined to finish it. The people in my degree and public relations classes were clever and captivating. I could always spot a comms classmate in the library because they'd be the one chatting people up and making them laugh. Many of them had a knack for motivating other students to get involved in whatever activity or event they were organising. I used to say that the art of public relations lies in the ability to present a shit sandwich and get others to not only talk about that sandwich, but want one themselves.

After finishing my degree, I set my sights on landing an internship at one of the biggest PR firms in the world. 'Thanks, Janika,' the interviewer said, shaking my hand afterwards. 'We'll contact you.' I hurried straight to the bathroom to look in the mirror and figure out who the heck that girl in the interview had been! Out of thin air, I'd summoned a confident, knowledgeable 22-year-old who'd nailed her pitch of, 'You need to hire me because I'm the person best suited for this role.' Without knowing it, I'd used storytelling power to create an outcome.

Against tough competition, I was selected for the internship, and from the very first day, I was in awe of the way the professionals around me could tailor a story to suit clients, journalists and peers. They knew how to get their way using language and presentation skills. When my internship was up, I wasn't ready to leave. I knew if I wanted to achieve the storyline I desired, I'd have to express myself authentically and effectively and let my bosses know how much I wanted to stay.

So, I did, and it worked! They opened up a new role for me and I went on to work with storytelling magicians to craft messages for brands including Netflix, Microsoft, and eBay. After years in this inspiring career, I decided it was time to pivot, and follow my heart. Today, I shepherd everyday storytellers like you towards the stories they truly want to live.

You're a storyteller, too

The sharing and consuming of stories is so deeply ingrained in our life that we are often oblivious to partaking in them from the minute we wake up till the minute we go to sleep. Don't believe me? Let me prove it to you.

Think of something as simple as your toothpaste. Why did you buy that particular brand? Is it familiar from your childhood? Perhaps Mum always brought an extra-large tube for family holidays and insisted the whole family shared it, and now you buy it because it reminds you of her. Were you motivated by pricing because you never pay more than $10 for toothpaste, convinced that all the bells and whistles they promise don't even work. (Your dad used to say the same thing.) Or maybe the ad you saw on TV made that brand stand out in this crowded aisle of squeaky clean. Maybe you saw the logo and started humming the ad's jingle as you reached to pick it up. We are motivated to make decisions based on effective storytelling, even for toothpaste.

We all have the same ability to elicit a desired response as any brand or ad, though this power often stays inside us because our culture tells us that effective storytelling is reserved for extroverts, leaders and people of influence with something important to say. Consequently, many of us struggle to feel worthy, noble or important enough to share our stories instead of realising that we have everything we need to express ourselves fully. We avoid sharing stories that are true and compelling, and miss out on the benefits of their persuasive power. Instead, we tell the same lacklustre stories as others so we don't rock the boat or stand out. Because of this, we collect missed opportunities – too asleep to recognise all the ways that expressing ourselves authentically might benefit our lives. It's time to reclaim that force and put it to use in every aspect of our lives where we share stories.

Areas such as:
- Connecting with family and loved ones.
- Making new friends.
- Winning over a sceptic.
- Persuading others to agree with you.
- Gathering support for a strategy.
- Delivering an engaging presentation.
- Nailing a job interview.
- Strengthening relationships with co-workers.
- Building trust with employees.
- Increasing client/customer satisfaction and retention.
- Securing a second date.

What if you could achieve all of these things while still being inherently you, just a stronger storytelling you? How could embodying that person and honoring your story improve your self-expression and life? That is precisely what this book is about. I'm going to show you how believing in your ability to tell your story will allow you to tap into that strength inside you and alter your life for the better.

Perhaps you're reading this book because you aren't sure what your story is. I can't tell you the number of times someone I'm working with says, 'I don't have any stories to tell.' They're always wrong, and if this sounds like you, I'm so glad you're here because, trust me, you have more power than you know. So, let's get started, storyteller!

Storytelling put simply

Let's start by demystifying the word 'storytelling'. Often, people are intimidated by what they think this entails. Flashback to year ten English class, and sweating buckets as you try to remember your oral assignment (public speaking can be triggering stuff, I know). But it's important to recognise that storytelling encompasses a diverse range of approaches and methods – it doesn't have to involve public speaking, though it can. Storytelling is simply expressing a narrative for a purpose – any purpose. Consider this: stories shared between friends and family 'just because' are still crafted and spread with a genuine desire for a specific outcome. Whether that outcome is as simple as eliciting laughter, providing affirmation, offering a reminder or fostering a connection, it is still driven by a purpose. We share narratives in a primal, instinctual way in order to understand and connect to ourselves as individuals and the world as a collective.

Steve Jobs once said, 'The most powerful person in the world is the storyteller', and rightly so because stories allow us to persuade, connect, motivate, heal, grow, build trust, teach and much more. They are so important that their billion-dollar industries have been constructed to support us sharing them. Storytelling transcends cultural and geographical boundaries, which is remarkable when you evaluate how constant this simple concept has remained.

I like to engage clients with this basic definition for the word storytelling, so it's easier to grasp within their everyday experiences, but I won't lie to you. I enjoy going deep (like deep-deep) with it, too, because storytelling, can also be sacred. Ritualistic expression can serve as a profound conduit connecting us to something greater than ourselves, and you best believe that's magic, too!

A story shared with heart and soul can help us step into the shoes of a protagonist and feel their pain, joy or fear as if it's our own. When a story captures our imagination, we hang on every word to find out how it ends, forgetting for a brief moment that it's not our own. Storytelling skill can be transformative not just for the storyteller, but also their audience by moving them deeply or motivating them in some way. Storytelling is a pure power that you have access to and already use in so many ways you may not even be conscious of.

Losing your voice

Our voice is undoubtedly our most important tool. It allows us to share our inner essence with the world by conveying our thoughts, feelings and ideas to others, so what happens if we lose our voice or it gets buried under layers of who we think we should be and how we think we should sound? Losing access to this vital tool is serious and can have detrimental consequences that inhibit our authentic expression. When we hold back from expressing ourselves, we rob ourselves of the opportunity to be fully seen, understood and heard by not only others, but also ourselves. We miss out on aligning with the stories we want to be part of when we don't speak up and claim them.

Can you recall a time when you were using your voice comfortably but then lost it because some dynamic shifted? Perhaps a colleague disagreed with your opinion in front of your boss and then you struggled to get your point across or lost all focus? Losing the power of your voice is a horrible feeling because it doesn't feel familiar.

You aren't yourself, and you don't feel secure enough to speak your truth. We've all had moments like this, and it's frightening because when we lose our voice, it can have significant consequences on our mental, emotional and physical wellbeing.

There are many reasons we might fall out of step out with our power and surrender our voice. Perhaps we're afraid of the consequences or conflict that speaking our truth might bring, and are afraid of being judged or rejected. Maybe we worry that our opinions and thoughts are not worthy of being heard, so we keep quiet. Perhaps we don't want to deal with the truth of our inner desires, so we continue to suppress them. Whatever the reason, when we withhold our storytelling power, we are only hurting ourselves because the only way to step into this power fully is to know and accept ourselves completely. If we don't, our self-worth, self-confidence and self-awareness continue to be eroded.

The trouble starts when we internalise inaccurate stories that support the narrative that our opinions don't matter, that we're not important enough or that we don't have control. This leads to a sense of powerlessness and a lack of agency in our lives which is downright exhausting in the long run and leads many of us down a rabbit hole until we're lost. Wondering, Who am I? How did I get here? What's next?

Silencing our self-expression doesn't just exact a mental toll; it takes a physical toll, too. The constant shoving down of our true stories puts the body in a perpetual state of fight or flight. Research shows that chronic stress, which can manifest from suppressing our thoughts and feelings, can lead to multiple health ailments like digestive problems, weakened immune systems and cardiovascular disease. I wasn't exaggerating when I said that sharing a story and expressing it in a powerful way can change your life, and also the health of your relationships and work life. When we fail to communicate in an honest, truthful and grounded way, we open ourselves up to misunderstandings, miscommunications and breakdown in relationships. Friendships may become strained because we're not communicating in a way that reflects who we truly are.

Make no mistake; you're not in your storytelling power just because you speak loudly or appear confident to your listeners. If you're not grounded in your truth and expressing from that place, you won't feel secure with your expression on the inside (and that is where it counts). Without truth, we deny ourselves the opportunity to be seen and heard for who we are. We miss out on stories that are meant for us and deprive others of the opportunity to get to know the real us and connect with us on a deeper level. To step into our power and regain our voices, it is essential we learn to use the power of our voice to direct our life story.

The science of stories

To understand the power of story, it's crucial to understand the impact quality storytelling has on our conscious and unconscious behaviours. When cognitive psychologist Jerome Bruner studied the power of stories, he observed that humans were 22 times more likely to retain facts if those facts were wrapped up and presented in a story. Just let that sink in. Twenty-two times more likely! Human brains are built to retain stories more easily than facts because we connect to them on an emotional level. Engaging with a story prompts our brains to release a cocktail of chemical neurotransmitters that solidify our affinity with that story. Here's a breakdown of this chemical cocktail.

Neurotransmitter	Purpose	Story type
Endorphins	Stress/pain reliever, increases wellbeing	Humorous or silly
Dopamine	Pleasure, satisfaction or motivation	Suspenseful cliff-hangers and mysteries
Oxytocin	Love, connection or bonding	Sad, romantic or wistful
Adrenaline	Fight, fright, or flight	Frightening, uncomfortable or irritating

What's even more remarkable is that stories don't just make us *feel* things, they also have the power to make us *do* things. Elevating endorphin levels in audience members can heighten their perception of pleasure and satisfaction and encourage the decisions they make afterwards. Dopamine significantly impacts focus and motivation, which engages an audience and can encourage them to act on a story's message. Oxytocin (also known as the love hormone) creates empathy and trust between the audience and the storyteller. It also causes a unique phenomenon called 'mirroring' whereby listeners of a story experience similar brain activity to the storyteller, and a true connection is formed. Storytelling manipulates our bodies to perform in a particular way. Even if you're not convinced that you are a storyteller quite yet, you will probably agree that you've experienced some of these sensations when hearing or watching a story. You may even be aware of having pulled the emotional strings of others through your storytelling. This was certainly the case for American writers Rob Walker and Joshua Glenn.

In 2009, Rob and Joshua set out to answer a question: how much more would people pay for an otherwise useless object if it had a good, emotional story tied to it? They collected 100 items– I'm talking useless, random, old items from New York City flea markets and thrift stores – clutter, essentially, such as a shot glass, kitty saucer and plastic banana. The aim was to sell these things on eBay for a profit. To do this, they engaged well-known writers to create short fictional stories to accompany each item for sale on eBay. On average, each item cost about $1.29, with the total for the collection coming in at $129. After selling all items on eBay, the total collection sold for (and this is the bit I had to read twice) $3,612.51! *checks notes* Yep, that's right. A 7,600 per cent markup as a direct result of the stories that had been created! I mean, a freaking shot glass sold for $76!

Their experiment is such a brilliant example of how storytelling can motivate us, and it became known as the Significant Objects Experiment. You don't need to be a neuroscientist to see that storytelling is in your makeup, or that anyone can benefit from knowing how to employ it.

Storyteller session 1:
How do you engage with storytelling in your life?

Welcome to your first storyteller session. You'll find these scattered throughout the book to provide you the opportunity for guided self-assessment. I encourage you to complete these exercises in order, though you can document your responses however you like. I enjoy journaling my thoughts in a special notebook I can refer back to. However, you may enjoy writing yours on a computer. Do whatever feels right for you.

Gentle reminder: This writing is just for you. You need not share it with anyone, so allow yourself space to answer honestly.

Be transparent and document whatever comes to mind without limiting your expression. Always ask yourself, Did my head or my heart answer that? My advice: lead with your heart when completing a storyteller session.

As we open our mind and expand our definition of storytelling to include our everyday interactions and experiences, see if you recognise any of the below methods of telling story in your own life.
- Posting or engaging on social media
- Chatting about my day with my loved ones
- Writing emails

- Making something with my hands
- Drawing or painting
- Watching movies and TV
- Listening to audiobooks and podcasts
- Attending meetings at work
- Calling friends on the phone
- Answering questions at the doctor's surgery
- Engaging in conversation with shop assistants at the checkout
- Journaling and reading
- Explaining myself or my business to others

Great! Now let's dig deeper. Reflect on any other ways you currently use or engage with stories in your daily life. As you begin to list them, you'll likely notice a trend in your favourite ways of expressing yourself. Perhaps you tend to express yourself through writing, speaking or drawing? Take stock of your natural preferences.

Now you have more insight into your typical storytelling methods, start answering these storyteller questions:

- Can you recall a time that you experienced losing your voice? What triggered this?
- Has a story ever spurred you to take action? What was that story and why did it resonate with you?
- Reflect on the stories you've told throughout your life that have helped you move forward in a desired direction? (Perhaps you told a story to land a dream job?)

CHAPTER TWO

You are the main character

My mother was and is one of the hardest workers I know. The woman is an absolute powerhouse, and I attribute a lot of my work ethic to 'get shit done' to the methods she taught me. Growing up, she was a 'working mum', the term coined for those who swapped full time stay-at-home mothering for jobs they either loved or hated depending on the day. You see, Mum was part of a generation of women sold the lie that they could have it all at once: career, marriage, home, children … the list went on. 'Equality' was the buzzword of the day, and the messaging that women could 'work like a man' was everywhere.

That promise of equality was, as Mum likes to say, 'all bullshit!' Fundamental issues like, oh, I don't know, the gender pay gap, childcare and overt sexism made achieving like a man nearly impossible. Turned out women had to work harder to juggle both domains, leaving them exhausted and taken advantage of, and with very little time to focus on their own stories or feel like a VIP in their own life because they were too busy taking care of everyone else.

This wasn't just my own mother's experience. Many women have shared stories about the realities of burnout in this 'have it all' culture that demanded so much of them all at once. Although my mother loved her career, she was absolutely buggered and rarely had time to consider any stories outside the ones she read to me at bedtime. One day, after a long slog at work, Mum came home, cooked dinner, cleaned up and then put me into my bed before collapsing into her own. She was tapped awake by yours truly. 'Mum. Hey, Mum.' I whispered.

Startled, she replied, 'What, Janika? What's wrong?!'

'I have a really important question. What's the meaning of life?' She stared at me for a few seconds and I thought *This is it. Mum's going to answer the question I've been thinking about all night.* Exhausted, frustrated and not in the slightest bit entertained, she grumbled, 'You go to work and you die. Now go to bed.'

Woah! I hightailed it out of her bedroom and jumped under my covers, thinking about the look in her eyes as those words left her mouth. The memory of that moment has never left me. Mum and I laugh our heads off about it today, and once she'd had a good night of sleep, she was able to give me a more appropriate response, but her moment of unfiltered honesty made a huge impact on me. Without knowing it, she'd given me a huge amount of clarity. I realised that when you don't take ownership of your role as the main character in your own life, you risk losing your inner fire and power to direct the most important story: your own.

The greatest story of all

Regardless of whatever religion, ideologies or philosophies we lean towards, the majority of us would probably agree that we feel called to follow a particular path or journey in life. It's this path that dictates the story of your life, and on a larger scale, the story of your journey is what remains when the physical body ceases to exist. The things you achieved, taught and shared, and the impact you had – positive and negative – stay with those you affected.

Your story relates to the satisfaction, passion and purpose you create in your day-to-day life. Having clarity on your existing story can assist you to evaluate whether it aligns with the direction you want your story to proceed in. Hopes, dreams, ambitions, values and more can filter into the vision for your life, and it's your human right to keep those fires fanned. Now, more than ever, people are struggling to find purpose. There are so many options and choices available and thanks to the conveniences of modern life, we live in a time where more of us than ever have the luxury of being able to ask, *What do I really want?*

This confusion about which path to follow can manifest in an array of mental and physical health blocks. If we don't know the why and the what of our stories, we can't express them in an authentic and powerful way. You'll understand this now you're aware of the *5 Steps to Storytelling Power.*

When author and owner of accessory and lifestyle brand Wilder, Sarah Wilder was a guest on my podcast, it was clear she was a woman who embodied this fire of self-knowledge. She knew herself so intimately that when I first heard her speak, the wild flames of her story, and the way she expressed it lit a spark in me. She described the journey she'd taken to accepting and becoming her authentic self in order to shift into the story she was always *supposed* to live.

Sarah had achieved an enviable career in high fashion and was living a life that, on the surface, seemed remarkable. But she wasn't satisfied. Something was missing and the story she was living felt far away from the person she was inside. One day, at work, she had a moment of clarity while looking at a ring on her finger: one her mum had given her. This special talisman instantly brought her back to the spiritual person and artistic creator she truly was, and reminded her of her passions for wildlife, philosophy, cosmology, astrology and more. In a flash of clarity, she realised that her current life wasn't supporting the truth of who she was as a person, or the things she cared about.

Shortly after reconnecting with her authentic self, Sarah left her cut-throat job and leaned into her truth, despite the challenges this big shift posed and the opinions of others. She understood that her real narrative was waiting for her if she had the confidence to pursue it. In the end, fashion remained part of her story, but in a way that suited her much better. Today, she's a jewellery designer creating beautiful talismans for people seeking their truth.

If you currently believe that you don't have control or choice over your story, I'm going to ask you to actively shift your thinking. It's true that life isn't fair and all of us have different challenges, but you do have the power to be the sole writer of your story. You may be hindered by self-doubt or feel you need more confidence to feel worthy enough to pursue the story you seek, but don't be afraid that it's too late to start owning your narratives. With every obstacle faced, a fresh perspective is born, and your story gains another foundational pillar that can be used in a powerful way when you follow the steps to express yourself. This book will help you see how all of the challenges, quirks, experiences and stories that make you uniquely you can provide the strength to express your true self.

Throughout this book, I refer to 'soul' or 'true self'. These terms mean slightly different things to different people; some may refer to soul as intuition, gut, heart, angel or inner self. For me, soul or true self refers to the inner essence of us that is all-knowing and connected to a higher consciousness. I don't mind what you call it. Go with whatever floats your boat. The most important thing is to tune into your true self so you can listen to what it's telling you, just as Sarah did.

The body keeps the score

Guess who gets dragged around for the ride no matter who is writing your story? Your body. If you're living in alignment with your soul and this true self is writing your story, you're more likely to feel healthy, nourished and energised from the inside out. This feeling of vitality is one of the most important feelings to engage with because it serves as your compass when making decisions. But if you're living a story that goes against your soul, your body keeps score, and by this, I mean it starts to suffer with physical symptoms like illness, discomfort or disease and causes you to experience mental, physical or emotional strain. You may be familiar with *The Body Keeps the Score*, the bestselling book by Bessel van der Kolk that explores the many ways the body holds and stores our secrets, lies and traumas. It's fascinating how traumatic experiences can shape our physical well-being and ultimately, our story. You might be able to manipulate your mind into believing you're fine by telling it a story that masks the truth, but you can't lie to your body. After a while, it will shout, 'Enough!' and rebel by making you run down, sick or tired.

I bring this up because learning this lesson has helped keep me majorly in (reality) check. I now pay attention to my body and the stories it is telling me before the symptoms develop further. How well do you listen to your body? When you're tired, do you rest? Imagine this: you're finally taking that holiday you've been dreaming of. The museum visits are planned, activities scheduled and restaurants you've been dying to stuff your face at are reserved. In the weeks leading up to the trip, you push yourself really hard to wrap up all your projects. Your body tries dropping hints all the way up to the departure date. It says, 'Hey, babe. You've got to take it easy this week. Don't overdo it on the overtime again. Go to bed early. Cancel that appointment. Say no to that lunch so you can rest.'

I'll be fine, Body. You think. *I can handle it.* You continue reassuring yourself as you ignore headaches, then a sore throat and a deepening purple tinge under your eyes. Upon landing at your destination, you get sick within hours of arriving at the hotel. Now, instead of enjoying that carefully planned itinerary you're forced to rest in bed with a book.

That's how it works. Your body will drop subtle hints long before it puts its foot down. It's been keeping track, regardless of whatever fictional narratives you've been telling yourself. It has a way of revealing the story you are *really* living – whether you like it or not.

When I was 20 and living with my parents, they called me into the kitchen for a 'talk'. This wasn't out of the ordinary. We were 'the Three Musketeers', an open-door, open-hearted family who shared everything with each other – or at least I thought we were before this talk blew the lid off our family unit and contradicted the honesty I felt we'd always enjoyed. My father explained that he'd had an affair, and consequently, a decision had been made and the outcome of that was not going to include the three of us being together anymore.

My mother was silent, more concerned with my feelings than her own. I don't remember much after Dad said his piece (funny how our brains block out certain stories), I just remember running as fast as I could to the empty park down the street. I needed to get outside – away from the artificial lighting, lies and our broken home. At 20, I was no longer a child, but the narrative of my family had been rewritten without my approval, and I didn't know how to handle that. I made the decision to put on a brave face for Mum's sake, and I tried my hardest to trick myself into believing everything was okay. I walked home, then spent the next few weeks robotically going through the transition period as my mother and I moved out of our family home. We were the Three Musketeers no more.

I stuck with my plan to override my painful loss of control with a fake sense of calm. Concerned friends and family marveled at my ability to carry on as if nothing was wrong. 'Staying strong' they called it, but my body – boy, did she have something to say. After months of me ignoring the signs that I was exhausted, devastated and barely hanging on, my body gave up on trying to clue me in. 'Ahh, yes.' My doctor said as he squinted to get a closer look at the burning rash that had erupted on the right side of my body. 'Shingles.

Quite common in over 50's, but rarer for someone your age.' He held my gaze for a little bit longer. 'Everything okay, Janika?' I'd trusted this doctor since I was little, and it was in his office that I burst into tears and the floodgates finally opened.

I told him everything, surprising myself with how much I'd bottled up and how much word vomit I was spilling onto my doctor's lap. I'd been so focused on acting out a story to protect my mum, my family (and myself to a degree) that I'd ignored the real story playing out inside my soul. Without storytelling as a tool to express my pain, my body was taking the story out of my hands to release it. My doctor let me finish before handing me a box of tissues along with a card to see a trusted colleague and psychologist. This wouldn't be the last time my body erupted in shingles, and it wouldn't be the last psychologist I saw, either, but it was a huge lesson that the truth of a story will find a way to express itself – one way or another. It took me a few times to learn this lesson properly, but these days I'm much better at listening to my body when it's trying to tell me a different story to the one playing in my mind.

How our narratives hold us back

You know the saying, *Keep your friends close and your enemies closer*? Well, I feel the same way about the stories we say aloud and those we tell ourselves. It's helpful to keep an eye on the types of narratives you're telling yourself because your internal dialogue is just as important as the one you express externally – maybe even more so. When that internal dialogue is negative (an 'enemy' if you will), it can hold you back in ways you might not even see.

Despite graduating high school with solid grades, I picked up a narrative that I was incapable of understanding maths, and I know the person who put that story in my head. In year four, little Janika was doing a bit too much socialising and not enough listening during maths. When it came time to take a test on the lesson we'd just reviewed, I blanked. From then on, my teacher directed snide comments my way: 'It's time for maths, Janika. Do you need to sit in a special chair so you can pay attention?' 'Maths really is not your subject.' And, 'Did you understand that, Janika? Or was it too advanced for you?' She made me feel embarrassed and ashamed, and chipped away at my confidence in this subject until eventually, it collapsed. I took her narratives, adopted them as my own, and held tight to them for years.

While studying psychology at uni, this old, poisonous narrative resurfaced, and tripped me up in a big way. I intended to go into clinical psychology because (big surprise) I was fascinated by human behaviour, brains and communication. I crushed my first few semesters of psychology and achieved the highest grades I've ever received. But lo and behold, I froze when faced with Statistics 01 – a required course.

I can't do this.
I'll fail. I'm not good at maths.
I've never been good with numbers.
This will be so embarrassing.

These stories played on a loop in my mind, and I heard nothing the lecturer said during that first class. The next day, I unenrolled, and not just from that stats class, but from the entire degree. I walked away from a path that may have brought me so much joy. Don't let a harmful narrative you tell hinder your ability to create the right ones.

What negative narratives do you tell?
Narrative: 'I'm not good at public speaking.'
How it manifests: Stops you from connecting with people by expressing your thoughts, emotions and messaging to an audience. You don't have to be the best public speaker in the world, but you DO have the right to express yourself. There will be times in your life when you are called on to speak (at weddings, funerals, or business opportunities) because you have something valuable to say.

Narrative: 'I'm the worst on first dates and super awkward.'
How it manifests: Prevents you from finding the right person because if you don't put yourself out there as the most genuine version of yourself, you will not be able to attract the right person for you. Be your damn awkward self!

Narrative: 'I'm lazy and have no drive.'
How it manifests: Stops you from looking deeper and examining why you're not drawing purpose from your current situation. It's not you, it's the vibe, so change that and watch 'laziness' turn into passion.

Why are we so freaking tough on ourselves? We would never be as rude, negative or hard on someone we care about, so why do we do it to ourselves? Usually, it comes down to fear: fear of embarrassment, fear of judgement, fear of failure. This was true for writer, Jess Kitching. During an interview with Jess, she shared how she struggled with the idea of judgement from others when it came time to release her debut novel out into the world.

Most of the time these were unconscious thoughts, but as the deadline from her publisher drew nearer, she was forced to overcome this narrative in order to move forward. She identified that even though it was frightening knowing a reader might look at her work and not enjoy it, it wasn't worth not pursuing her dream of becoming a writer. Doing this enabled her to 'get on with it' and put it all out there.

A large part of our journey is coming face-to-face with the stories we tell ourselves, then holding them up to the light so we can see the reality of them and determine whether they are serving or hindering us. Identifying and evaluating your current narratives is a crucial first step to harnessing your storytelling power.

If our lives are a story, then it's safe to say they follow a plot that includes our past, present and future. This timeline shapes our thoughts, habits and behaviours, and has a fundamental effect on the direction of our lives. That said, it's essential to understand the importance of balance in this plot we are putting our energy into. Spending too much time in the past can erode the belief that you can direct future stories. If I allowed that negative story about maths to dictate my future, that story would become: *I've always been bad at maths in the past, so I'll always be bad at it.*

Similarly, spending too much time thinking of the future can also hinder your ability to live in the present. *I must get this job with the company I've always dreamed of working for. Even though I've been offered another opportunity, I'm not going to consider it.*

Soon, we'll explore how to use the past to create a foundation for the present and enables you to express yourself efficiently as you move towards your desired future.

Uncover the stories worth sharing

At this point, it's vital I remind you how important your individual story is. Earlier I mentioned that in my career as a professional storyteller, clients often say, 'I don't have a story'. If they're an entrepreneur, they may be happy to share information about the product or service they offer, but when it comes down to attaching their personal story to that brand, business or product, they struggle. My response is always the same – that every single one of us has many stories worth telling.

If you find it hard to know which story to express, ask yourself the following questions: What is the story you most want to share? A learning? A formative experience? A comfort? A time when you had a positive impact? Which stories do you want to leave behind when you die? This might be a tad morbid, I'll admit, but there's nothing like the thought of death to encourage a person to start sharing their truth. I know this because a brush with death forced my own truth to surface.

After enduring a long, exhausting (and masked-up thanks to COVID) labour with my second child, I was told his umbilical cord was wrapped around his neck, and that I'd need to have an emergency C-section. During the operation that followed, I hemorrhaged, losing two of my five litres of blood. I danced in and out of consciousness as my husband held my hand. When I woke, a nurse placed my baby on my chest to feed. I was dazed, and couldn't shake the knowledge that my life had nearly ended. Experiences, learnings and insights from my life started bubbling to the surface, and I gained a huge amount of clarity on the wisdom I'd gained from the past, and the direction I wanted to pursue in the future. I channeled that clarity into these five steps. Hopefully, it won't take a life-threatening experience for you to understand your story's power.

When asking clients to consider the narratives they're called to share, another thing I commonly hear is, 'I don't feel I have the authority to share or claim it.' This couldn't be further from the truth! You are the expert when it comes to your life. Nobody else has the same perspective, experience or circumstances as you, and it's this unique viewpoint that gives you the authority to speak on what you know. You don't have to be a psychologist to speak about trauma. If you are, then you'll approach the topic from your professional perspective, but if you're someone who has lived through trauma, then lived experience will be the approach you take. The lens through which you are sharing your story is the thing that allows you to take ownership of it and grants you the authority to speak on it.

Mercedes Mercier is a fantastic example of how incredible it can be when you use your own story and lived experience as the authority. When Mercedes first set out to become an author, she wanted to write romance (which she would have been brilliant at, no doubt), but when the words didn't flow as easily as she hoped they would, she felt deflated. While discussing this frustration with a mentor of hers, they pointed out that the years she'd spent working in the criminal justice system gathering information about prisons, crime and offenders might give her a real edge when it came to writing in the crime genre. They were right! She'd been sitting on a gold mine of real-life experience without even realising it. Mercedes pivoted to crime, and her unique lens took her storytelling to a level most could never achieve. Her crime manuscript was picked up by a major publisher, and she has since released book number two.

What happens when we share?

Expressing your narrative, in whatever form suits you, is worth investing in because when you share your stories, it has so many benefits, and can help you grow, heal, release, connect, represent, educate, motivate and so much more.

I've experienced each and every one of these benefits while engaging in my own expression and hearing others express themselves. Representation, in particular, is something that's had an enormous impact on my life. Growing up, I tried to downplay my heritage. As one of the only mixed-race kids in my suburban Brisbane neighbourhood, I desperately wanted to fit in and be 'normal'. Who I was wasn't represented in the world I saw around me, so when looking around for role models who looked like me, I'd grab on to identities that seemed somewhat similar whenever I'd catch glimpses of them in mainstream media. My father is African–American with Native American heritage, while Mum is Irish–Australian. In the early 2000s, our mixed family and my coloured skin invited a whole bunch of questions. 'Is that your mum?' 'Are you adopted?' 'Why is your grandma white?' 'Is your dad Eddie Murphy?'

Brisbane in the 90s and early 2000s wasn't exactly what I'd call diverse, so these questions usually came from a place of confusion, not malice. Even so, they made me shrink and increased my desire to turn down the volume of my voice and assimilate. Turning down the volume of my afro hair turned out to be quite tricky, especially with no black women in my newsfeeds, emails or search results. I could type *How to look after curly hair* into Google, but the storytelling just was not there. Representation was lacking in mainstream media, and my self-esteem suffered because of that. I'd spend hours crying about not having straight silky hair then force myself to smile politely when a girl at school would yank my curls, laughing, 'It feels like sheep hair. Yuck!'

As I grew older, I'd get the classic, 'Hey look, it's Beyoncé!' (I mean, I *wish* I looked like Queen B but I'm not that delusional.) But kids were only calling me by her name because she was one of few women of colour on TV at that time. It's not that storytelling about women of colour wasn't happening anywhere, it just wasn't as available to me in Queensland, Australia.

It's imperative to mention that, historically, not all storytellers have had the same platform, but as the cry for diversity grows louder and the gatekeepers continue to shift, there are more and more microphones available. We have a long way to go before diverse stories are represented equally across storytelling mediums, but the fact that I can now turn on the TV and have my daughter see herself represented in stories and by people on all sorts of platforms has a profound and positive effect on me. I'm proud of my heritage and its stories, and now I've also learned a thing or two from #curlyinstagram!

The power is within you

We've talked about the principal aspects of storytelling, its profound effects and how each of us has something to share. If this were an average storytelling book, it would probably end here, with some strategies on how to pretend to be something you're not so you can deliver a kick-ass business presentation and secure top-tier clients. However, that's not the point of this book, and I have a much more significant message to share with you – one sure to stick with you longer than a memorised presentation. My message is simple:

You already have this storytelling power within you.

What's more, you don't need permission, expensive storytelling courses or 100,000 followers on social media to use it. And you certainly don't need a trendy hairstyle or expensive outfit to share stories that can impact other people. I'll show you how to use storytelling power to harness and share your true stories, as you are right this very minute, in a way that benefits your life.

Once we open our awareness to the fact that storytelling is everywhere and accept that our unique voice holds weight, we gain the ability to control the narratives in our lives by overcoming challenges, communicating correctly, directing our self-talk, and pursuing the narratives we truly desire. The ability to tap into your storytelling power is already within you, and after implementing these five steps, I guarantee you'll arrive back at the truth of who you are feeling more confident and surer of yourself when you express your truth, in whichever medium you choose. It's time to take charge of your life by directing the narratives within it.

Storytelling session 2:
Embrace your VIP status

Keeping the ideas we've explored in this chapter in mind, tick the statements you agree with below (answer truthfully!).

- ☐ I understand that my life is the most important story I can create.
- ☐ I listen to my body when it tries to tell me something.
- ☐ I'm aware of the good, bad and ugly stories that I tell myself.
- ☐ I believe I have at least one story worth sharing.
- ☐ I've been positively affected when other people have shared their stories and grasp the importance of them doing so.

By understanding and agreeing with these statements, you're making a commitment to yourself to value not only your story, but also the reality that every one of us has a valuable narrative to tell. We're all worthy of embracing the VIP status in our own life.

5 STEPS TO STORYTELLING POWER

Now it's time to access your power and create positive action aligned with the story that is your life. Turn the page and prepare to step into your storytelling power as we walk through these five life-changing steps together. After each one, we'll look at practical ways to apply it to three key areas where storytelling matters: work, relationships, and the relationship we have with ourselves.

CHAPTER THREE

Step 1: Making space for your narratives

'When we have the courage to walk into our story and own it, we get to write the ending.'[1]
Brené Brown, *Professor and Author*

I remember exactly where I was when I heard this quote from American research professor, author and speaker, Brené Brown. It stopped me in my tracks while cooking dinner one night. I was listening to her audiobook, and felt so inspired by her words that I stopped stirring the tomato and basil pasta sauce (my specialty, btw). Brené is a master at translating her research on shame, vulnerability and leadership in an honest and relatable way. She intertwines storytelling with science so effectively that this has become her trademark style and cemented her as a leading thought leader. Her ideas certainly stick with me.

Often, self-help messaging is centred around the individual forging a new path and going at it full force – ignoring or setting aside their past to build a new future. I don't buy that approach! As someone who works with people daily, I constantly witness the differences between storytellers who are aware of their past stories and those who ignore them completely.

I have observed that people who are clear on how their past influences their present typically have a more profound understanding of how powerful owning their past can be. I'm not just talking about the positive stories, either. Owning failures, setbacks and pain from the past can be just as powerful as the good stories if you know how to use those to move forward. That's why it was refreshing to hear Brené say that the past is an invaluable piece of our story – one we either hold as a strength or reject completely.

Hence why the first step to stepping into your storytelling power is knowing where you've come from because making space for your narratives creates the foundation for your potential. It can feel frightening to revisit stories of hurt, failure, and pain, but, my friend, there is no easy way to avoid them. As we saw in chapter two, past stories already live inside us. They'll find a way to express themselves one way or another, so let's consider a braver approach.

Owning all of our stories means acknowledging our feelings and understanding that the narratives (good and bad) we take away from our experiences continue to affect us today. It's when we say, 'This is who I am because of that experience. Hear me roar!' that we take the first step to elevating our storytelling. Without an authentic foundational structure, our stories lack backbone. We must embrace who we've been until this point to direct the next chapter of life.

With this in mind, let's identify the stories currently playing in your life. After, we can investigate how your past has informed them, with or without your knowledge.

The narrative of now

As born storytellers, we live our lives based on stories we've either made up or been told about how the world works. These unconscious narratives become our default setting, and they often go unchallenged as we carry on making blind statements such as, 'Bad things always happen to me.' 'Trouble always finds me,' or 'I'll always be broke.' Without realising it, we trap ourselves in that very narrative by repeating these stories. To uncover the script you are currently engaging with, let's look at nine story archetypes and unpick the narratives within.

Archetype 1: Rags to riches

This narrative involves the experience of coming from a low position in society and rising to a position that is valued (by the individual or society), often through hard work and determination. When a person rises from a life of extreme poverty to one of extreme wealth or status, this change is perceived as positive.

Example: Chris Gardner, despite a disadvantaged background, overcame homelessness and financial struggles to achieve remarkable success. His inspiring journey from the streets to becoming a successful stockbroker and entrepreneur was portrayed in the movie *The Pursuit of Happyness*.

Statements in this script:
- *'I've come a long way.'*
- *'I've worked hard to be in a better place.'*
- *'I'll never go back.'*

Archetype 2: The underdog

In this story, everyone doubts the underdog's ability to achieve what they want. They constantly have to work harder than others to gain recognition or success. The underdog typically wins in the end, taking everyone by surprise.

Example: In the movie *Legally Blonde*, pretty, fashionable California girl Elle Woods faces discrimination at Harvard because of her appearance and personality. She struggles to convince her bookish peers and teachers that she has the smarts to study law. Most people underestimate her, but she proves them wrong while stating that women can do and wear whatever they want (go, Elle!).

Statements in this script:
- *'I showed them.'*
- *'I gave it my all.'*
- *'I proved them wrong.'*

Archetype 3: The tragedy

Captures the painful and sad continuation of stories that ultimately lead to a tragic event. The tragic event can also symbolise being stuck in a harmful loop.

Example: Amy Winehouse – an exceptionally talented young singer – had her career and life cut short by an alcohol and drug addiction that ultimately took her life.

> **Statements in this script:**
> - *'I can't help it.'*
> - *'I have no control.'*
> - *'I'm on a path to destruction.'*

Archetype 4: The quest

This narrative represents the desire to travel, search and take risks in order to find what you're looking for. The central lesson often showcases that the journey is just as important as the destination.

Example: In the animated move *Finding Nemo*, an uptight (fish) father risks it all to find the son that has been taken from him. Along the way, he meets colourful characters who make his experience memorable and fulfilling.

> **Statements in this script:**
> - *'I'll search until I meet my goal'.*
> - *'It won't happen overnight.'*
> - *'I've learned so much.'*

Archetype 5: The comedy

An entertaining narrative that revolves around humour. It celebrates someone who keeps things light and sees the brighter side of life, sometimes at their own expense.

Example: In *Deadpool*, main character, Wade Wilson (aka Deadpool), filters his pain and uncomfortable topics through a prism of comedy, giving the outward impression that he takes life less seriously than others.

Statements in this script:
- 'I just laugh it off.'
- 'It's not that serious.'
- 'I don't care.'

Archetype 6: The rebirth

In this narrative, we witness the personal growth of a character as they transform from who they were into who they were meant to be.

Example: In television series *Game of Thrones*, the character of Sansa Stark evolves throughout the course of the series. Though the circumstances that initiate this personal transformation are terrible, they force her to leave behind the passive, obedient girl she once was and become the strong, leading lady she was always meant to be.

Statements in this script:
- 'I've changed.'
- 'I'll never be the same again.'
- 'I've become the person I was destined to be.'

Archetype 7: The romance

A story focused on a romantic relationship or love affair where two people are drawn together (for better or worse), leaving a noticeable mark on their life.

Example: The famous play *Romeo and Juliet* embodies the essence of this narrative, portraying a passionate love affair (forbidden in this case). Born into feuding families, two star-crossed lovers showcase the power of love and romance in adversity, and make the ultimate sacrifice to be together.

> **Statements in this script:**
> - 'My love for you knows no bounds.'
> - 'I'll never love like this again.'
> - "We were written in the stars.'

Archetype 8: David and Goliath

In this story archetype, a little guy (David) takes on the big guy (Goliath), representing how someone with less power than another can channel bravery, go head-to-head with a giant in battle, and succeed against the odds.

Example: Erin Brockovich, a single mother from Kansas with no formal law education joins a small-town law firm as an assistant then discovers that a large multinational corporation's negligent practices are poisoning the town's family. Though the company tries to cover it up, Erin is instrumental in pursuing the case and wins the largest settlement ever paid in a direct-action lawsuit in US history despite having far fewer resources and influence than the multinational.

Statements in this script:
- *'I'm not afraid of them.'*
- *'Nothing can stop me.'*
- *'I'll stop them.'*

Archetype 9: The revenge

A wronged person seeks retribution from those who have crossed their boundaries, betrayed or harmed them in some way.

Example: Keanu Reeves character in the popular John Wick movies showcases a journey of revenge against those who have wronged him in the complex world of gangsters and assassins. Devastated by the murder of his beloved dog Daisy, he seeks vengeance to make those responsible for her death pay.

Statements in this script:
- *'I'll stop at nothing.'*
- *'What goes around comes around.'*
- *'I'll make sure they pay.'*

Which example resonates with you the most? There's no right or wrong answer; one plot line isn't better or worse than the others. Perhaps a few of them spoke to you. Have another read through these plot archetypes and identify any you feel best describe your current story. After you've done this, take a few minutes to get honest about the plot you've aligned with and make a note of why you think that is the case. If you struggle to see your life story in one of these plot archetypes, let's try something slightly different. What if your life were a movie?

Which part are you playing?

What's your favourite movie? I know mine. Here, I'll give you some clues: the title is two words. Starring Cameron Diaz and Kate Winslet … are you getting warmer? One lives in sunny LA, the other in wintery England. Oh, it's on the tip of your tongue, isn't it? If you guessed *The Holiday*, you win! It's a rom com from 2006 about two women with guy problems who do a house swap at Christmas time. I know many people who identify with Cameron Diaz's storyline in this film, but Kate's character, Iris, is the one I relate to, and this was especially true throughout my 20s.

Like Iris, I worked late nights in a media job and wasted time crying over a complete ass who wasn't worth a single one of my tears. I also befriended wise people and made kind friends who taught me about true love. Ah, I loved Iris's open heart in this film, and the way she shared it with so many despite it being broken.

In one scene, after Iris shares her current narrative with a retired screenwriter, he leans in and says, 'Iris, in the movies we have leading ladies, and we have the best friend. *You*, I can tell, are a leading lady, but for some reason, you are behaving like the best friend'. Finally, this truth clicks for her, and she breathes, 'You are so right. You're supposed to be the leading lady of your own life, for God's sake!' Bingo, buddy!

Iris is spot on! We should be the main character of our own movie. And I don't mean this in a superficial #maincharacterenergy kind of way. I mean it to highlight that we should be moving through life with agency and a healthy amount of control. Ideally, we should be able to put things in perspective, see where we've come from and go after the story we desire because it is ours. Don't like the plot archetype that you connected with earlier? Empower yourself to change your perspective and create a better narrative.

One of the main reasons people find themselves unsatisfied with their present situation is that they feel like they aren't directing their own stories. They feel trapped and unable to create new scenes, and this feeling of being stuck creates a fear that who they are will inevitably be who they will become. True strength comes from evaluating the movie of your life so far and drawing strength from the scenes that have given you the authority to step into your leading energy.

You will never be stuck if you can hold on to the belief that this is *your* movie to direct and star in. It's your name in lights on the marquee, so knowing where you came from and what your stories have been are essential to this step. Ask yourself, what kind of movie are you currently living in? Who have you become because of that? Are you the main character or the best friend? What movie would you rather be living in?

Where you put your energy matters

As important as it is to reflect on how you've been living and which stories you've been involved in, it's also important to accept that sometimes you won't get to call all the shots or direct every scene. We live in the real world, with billions of other people and flawed structures and systems, so our stories are often influenced by love; finances; social events; our physical, mental and spiritual energy; or creativity. It would be unrealistic to think we can control *all* aspects of our story *all* of the time.

One thing we can usually control, though, is where we focus our attention and direct our precious energy. This next activity will help you identify the areas of life you're dedicating the most energy and chapters to. There are bound to be factors you can't control influencing the spread of your energy, but it's essential to understand where the majority of your attention goes and reflect on why that is.

An easy way to calculate how much of your story is tied up in a particular category is to do just that: make a calculation. Look at the list of categories below and write down what percentage of your time you dedicate to each one. (Make sure the total adds up to 100 once you're done.)

Work: Career. Service. Contribution. Responsibility. ___ %

Love: Relationships. Friends. Family. ___ %

Finances: Assets. Resources. security. ___ %

Social: Connection. Fun. Community. ___ %

Physical: Exercise. Rest. Nutrition. ___ %

Mental: Wisdom. Learning. Well-being. ___ %

Spiritual: Expansion. Soul. Truth. ___ %

Creativity: Adventure. Play. Inspiration. ___ %

How did you go? Did anything here surprise you? Are you happy with the percentage of your life being dedicated to each category? If not, at least you understand what your current story is. In order to change, we first have to be aware of what it is we wish to alter or rebalance in our stories. Many contributing factors have influenced your stories, now it's time to unravel why that may be the case.

Challenge your old stories

I once saw a psychic (so many good stories start with those words), and she was brilliant. Immediately, she picked up on my mentality around hard work, but not to give me a pat on the back. She wanted to help me tear down a story – the one that said I had to work hard my whole life in order to be of worth. Miraculously, she even managed to replace it with a story I *truly* believed. When I permitted myself to explore this narrative, I discovered that I didn't actually believe work had to be hard (all of the time). What I really believed was that it could be an enjoyable way to release my creativity and expression, which are equally as worthy as hard work. I left that reading with her a thousand times lighter, and I couldn't help wondering where the hell that narrative had come from. How long had it been with me? How many ways had it held me back? It obviously wasn't my own story, so how did it get inside me and stick? The answer, as it often is, is conditioning.

From day one we are conditioned by the people and cultures around us to hold certain beliefs. We ingest the stories of others, digest them as our own then permit those beliefs to form the basis upon which we tell the story of who we are to ourselves and others. So much of self-perception is shaped by childhood, and piece by piece, our collection of stories constructs a coat of armour over our soul. This becomes the persona we present to the world. The people we meet, education we do or don't get, places we live and societal pressures all add additional layers of steel onto this armour, masking our true self so we can 'fit in'.

These added layers of complexity (commonly referred to as the effects of conditioning) and learned behaviours inhibit us from expressing our authentic selves, and thus alter the course of our narratives. If we want to shed the heavy armour weighing us down, we have to examine and question these layers.

While I believe education is incredibly important, there's no denying that the way we are conditioned during our school years plays a big part in how we interact with institutional structures as adults. It's human nature to crave connection and a sense of belonging to a tribe. We take cues from our experiences and peers when looking to assimilate. It's not until we peel back those layers of this conditioning that we think, *Hang on a second, do I really believe this?* We've been consuming the stories of our culture since birth. Now it's time to pause and evaluate how that has affected your story to date.

Can you think of any expressions you heard when you were young? Perhaps you were told things like 'You're not a hard worker unless you're the first in, and last out every day.' Or 'Nothing comes easily'. These sayings may have instilled the belief in you that in order to achieve, you had to always work hard. Explore your own conditioning and write a list of sayings and their consequential beliefs.

Storyteller session 3:
Challenge your conditioning

It's important to understand how conditioning has influenced the story you are currently telling. Reflect on the questions below then write out your thoughts to see if they reveal any insights.

- What sayings did you commonly hear when you were growing up?
- Where did you hear them? Who said them?
- Can you identify any fears you developed because of these sayings?
- How have these fears limited you?
- Can you see how this belief or story has affected the trajectory of your life story?
- Have you come across evidence that goes against this conditioning?
- What belief would you like to replace this fear with?
- Have you come across evidence that affirms this new belief that you want to have?

The purpose of this session is not to make you feel bad for ingesting the conditioning – it's impossible to avoid. As children, we trust those who care for us, and with that blind trust comes blind faith that everything they teach us is, indeed, correct. Evaluating beliefs we've formed as a result of our conditioning can provide so much insight into why we've been who we've been, and assist us to create a better foundation for the future. Knowledge is power.

Uncover the gems in your timeline

Now that you've identified the type of narrative you've been living and explored the reasons your life may have followed this narrative, the next phase of holding space involves interrogating *why* that has been the case (this is my favourite part). Most people find this part of step one the most challenging, particularly if they've never evaluated their life from a bird's-eye view. Life is busy, and unless we carve out time and space to live consciously, it's easy to fall into the trap of just *existing* and thinking that all things happen to us for no reason.

Thinking you have no control over what you take from a situation or experience is not a correct assumption. Valuable gems of wisdom and insight have already formed from your past experiences. Much like a diamond, they've developed from pressure, but also from learnings and observations.

These insights inform the 'why' that you can use to anchor your present-day storytelling. Beautiful gems born from your stories. Sounds heavenly, right? The problem is that sourcing these gems can be difficult. We become forgetful, life gets busy, and these treasures get a little dusty. Finding your gems requires sifting through a lot of mental and emotional clutter. I always advise people to start by looking for those moments they felt most like themselves, or the version of the self they want to become. Perhaps you'll land on a big fat 'A-ha moment', or maybe you'll recall moments that clarified things. Remember these revelations. They are gems, too!

Depending on your experience, particularly around hardship narratives, you may not uncover a 'why did this happen' sort of gem, but you may discover a 'why I will go on' gem, which is equally as important. A dear client – I'll call her Tash – needed gem-dusting badly. As we started our session, I couldn't help noticing that Tash looked stressed. This girl was freaking exhausted. In addition to the daily grind of parenting small children, running a home and owning her own business, Tash was experiencing some challenges in her relationship. By her own account, her husband was kind, affectionate and let her take the lead in the relationship, but increasingly they'd been butting heads (as parents of newborns often do). She confessed she was feeling frustrated with him and 'touched out', partially from his efforts to connect with her.

Tash felt lost about what she needed to do next to improve this feeling and show up more in her relationship. I said, 'Girl, I've got you. You already know what to do. You just need to dust off one of your gems.' I got out my little imaginary duster and started walking her back through the timeline of her life with her husband. We revisited stories from before they became parents. It's funny how going through these motions can make someone remember lessons they've already learned.

While walking through this process, Tash revealed that this wasn't the first time she'd had trouble connecting with her husband. (Tash's gem was nearly in plain sight!) They'd called it quits once before because she felt he was too dependent and devoted, only once she was single again did Tash realise why she felt this way about her loving, caring partner. The relationships she'd had with men before her husband had all been toxic – full of manipulation, cheating and lies. After those relationships, she'd vowed that her forever partner would be someone who embodied a caring, soft and affectionate nature.

Uncovering this gem reminded Tash that her husband *was* exactly all of those things she'd looked for, and what she truly wanted in a partner. Luckily, he took her back. As I helped her blow the specs of dust off this piece of wisdom, she said, 'I'm too hard on him for being exactly what I asked for. He's kind and loves me exactly how I want to be loved, and now it's time I show him some love back'. Gem uncovered!

***

I've dusted off several of my own gems over the years. Another way to describe this process is the popular expression *Hindsight is 20/20*. The past can reveal so much about why you are who you are today. My favourite gems are the ones that appear when you zoom out and look at your life from that bird's-eye-view. From this vantage point, the gems you need are way more visible – you'll spot them glinting under a bush. They show themselves when you most need them with an almost magical synchronicity, and once you spot them, you'll think, *Ah, yes! That makes perfect sense. Of course, I had to learn that lesson to get here.* And suddenly, you'll know exactly what you need to do.

As challenging as gems are to form and collect, every one is valuable. You can add each one to your structure of the past and use them to elevate your storytelling – highlighting the wisdom you've accumulated from past chapters. To help you dust off your gems now, answer the following questions:

- Has a past experience taught you something about yourself, the world, your family or yourself?
- When did a choice you make turn out to be the wrong/right one?
- Has an object, place or person that meant a lot to you nearly destroyed you?
- Has had a negative experience taught you something invaluable? What did you learn?

So long as you come through each chapter of your life with these gems of learnings and truths to help you navigate the rest of your path, you'll have useful tools to upskill your storytelling.

Storyteller session 4:
Dust off your gems

Specific memories will stand out when evaluating your life as a timeline, and the learnings are bound to shine through. To assist you discovering your gems, Work through the prompts below.

1. Write down a timeline of your life, noting key events and memories that stick out to you.

2. Which stories from your life do you notice yourself telling when you make a new friend?
3. What are the stories your friends/family always encourage you to share?
4. With the stories from questions 2 and 3 in mind:
   - How do you feel about sharing them?
   - Do you ever adjust them? If so, why?
   - How do people react when you do share them?
5. Which stories in your timeline do you keep hidden? Why?
6. Pick the five most influential stories in your timeline that have changed the course of your life somehow.
   - What did you decide/learn/do after living through each of these stories?
   - Which decisions have been the hardest or easiest to live with?
   - How do your 'top-five' stories continue to influence your narratives today?

Exploring these prompts should bring your gems to the surface, as it's typically through these influential and memorable stories that they are created. Once you understand how your narratives have given you a valuable perspective, you can use them as the base of your future storytelling power. But to do this, you'll have to identify them and claim them as your own.

Your experiences are what give you authority

Memory lane can be challenging place. Sure, the fuzzy, joyful moments stay with us forever, but so do all the not-so-warm prickly ones. When we endure heartbreaks, hard lessons or devastating blows, it's hard to grasp why we have to endure them, even if we understand that it will eventually produce a gem. I circle back to fate, which the Oxford English Dictionary defines as 'That which is destined or fated to happen'. I find it interesting to discuss this concept with people because, how they view this word often influences how they view their own narratives. When a client and I get to the topic of fate and destiny, those who feel slighted by fate instantly get their backs up and say things like, 'It's not real. I don't believe in it.' And 'I believe in free will.'

Don't get me wrong, I believe in free will, too. But fate and free will are not mutually exclusive. I believe that some experiences are predetermined (fate), while some happen *because* we've exercised free will and selected a path to travel. I believe we make these choices because they lead to an experience we are destined to have. This can be a confronting idea for some – particularly if they've experienced hardship. Bad things happen to good people. It isn't fair, and sometimes bad things can be downright horrific and have catastrophic consequences. Nevertheless, I still believe that some of our experiences are fated to happen because they make us who we are destined to become. That said, it is ultimately our choice when we choose to follow a certain path or turn to another.

When author Jess Kitching explained her narrative to me, weaving her past through her present, and then looking to her future, what blew me away was that it was so clear to me that she was supposed to go through what she had endured to become the woman she is today. Jess was born with a large, strawberry-sized birthmark on her forehead and experienced relentless bullying because of it. My mouth dropped to the floor as she described the mockery and cruelty she experienced as a child. Classmates would throw things at her head while laughing and tormenting her. She was made to feel small and embarrassed by this thing she could not change and had to endure comments like, 'You're so brave going out of the house looking like that.' And 'Have you been hit on the head?' 'She's the ugly Jess.'

Instead of letting this challenging childhood break her, Jess claimed all of her stories and channelled everything she'd learned from being the victim of bullying into one of her biggest dreams: becoming a published author. She wrote a brilliant thriller with a twisted ending that spoke to the legacy of the trauma of bullying. Today, she looks at her birthmark and the narrative around it as something that taught her the value of self-acceptance and inspired her to create her popular novels. She's just released her second book, and will be writing multiple books in the future, at her publisher's request.

This example is precisely what this aspect of step one is about. Claim your past stories, then use them to ground you in the stories you share today. Those give you the authority to speak on a particular topic from your unique perspective. When you share a story through the lens of your true, lived experience, your soul is protected because no matter how your story is interpreted by others, it's a true expression of you.

Here are other examples of how a difficult past narrative might give a storyteller authority in the present day.

- Experiencing a heartbreaking divorce might give someone the tools to help others who've been blind-sided by their partner to create a plan of action and move on with their lives.
- Grief after losing a mother could be channelled into creating a community of grievers and leading them through the process as they connect over this common loss and struggle with modern-day grief.
- A survivor of an emotionally abusive relationship will be better equipped to point out red flags to a friend dating someone displaying dangerous traits.
- Someone who survives cancer might use their storytelling power to provide hope to others and help them overcome fear and see the importance of maintaining positive mental health throughout their journey.

The contents of this chapter will hopefully have helped you focus your thinking on the stories you've experienced in your life and how they've influenced your story to date. Reviewing your narratives, no matter how big or small, helps you understand their role in your life so you can weave them into your present and future stories in a useful way that benefits you.

Applying step 1 in real life

Now that we've shed light on your perspectives, claimed your stories and dusted off some gems, let's explore how you can put those learnings to use in your daily life.

WORK

Whether you own your own business or you're an employee, sharing a story from your past or providing insight into why you have the perspective you do can help you build credibility, deepen relationships and even help others see themselves in your story. The following situation and application demonstrate how you can use your stories to your advantage in the context of your business or career and elevate the way you are storytelling.

Building credibility

Sara Blakely, the founder of Spanx, is a fantastic example of someone who built credibility in business by sharing a story from her past. Sara faced an uphill battle attempting to launch her revolutionary line of shapeware for women. As a female entrepreneur in a predominantly male-dominated industry, she endured skepticism and resistance from industry peers and potential investors. To break down these barriers and establish that she had the credibility to be in the game, she shared a powerful story from her past.

When pitching her product to investors and buyers, Sara opened up to them about the personal struggles she faced while trying to find affordable, comfortable yet effective shapeware to wear under a pair of white pants. Feeling frustrated by the lack of choices, she described how she cut the feet off a pair of pantyhose and wore them as a solution. This was the driving force that inspired her idea to develop a product that offered a more comfortable alternative. By sharing this past experience, Sara demonstrated to potential investors that she understood the target market's need and had the credibility to position herself as the problem solver. Sara went on to use this personal anecdote as part of the brand narrative for Spanx. By leveraging her personal experiences, she was able to establish herself as a titan of the shapewear industry.

Real-life application: Creating credibility in a job interview
Here are five tips on how to create credibility in a job interview by making space for your narratives.

1. **Preparation**

    Research the company and job description beforehand to create a list of the main aspects of the role they would expect you to have credibility on. Once listed, prepare relevant stories and identify key experiences from your past that demonstrate your skills and showcase your expertise in that particular area.

2. **Practice**

    Before the interview, practice telling your stories aloud to become comfortable with the delivery. Ask your friends and family if you can practice with them and have them provide constructive criticism to assist your storytelling.

3. **Show confidence**

    During the interview, you'll want to watch your body language, tone and pace to make sure you're appearing calm, relaxed and informative. These are your stories, and these are your experiences, so stand strong in that.

4. **Structure your stories**

    Create a structure for your stories so that they flow naturally. Begin by describing or acknowledging the situation, then detail your specific task or goal within it, explain the actions you took and why and then end with the results and why you feel confident to handle the situation.

5. **Provide specific details**

    Remember, you'll want to stick to specific details so that you don't lose your audience (or interviewers) attention. Provide relevant stories from your past and demonstrate how they make you a credible, perfect fit for the role.

RELATIONSHIPS

The past can hold valuable insight when it comes to our relationships with others. How well you are able to express your past can help others understand where you're coming from and allow you to build a deeper connection with them. It's natural to use the past as a point of reference for our present, and it's common for people to behave a certain way or believe a particular thing as a result of their history.

Raiding your memory bank is an incredible tool when building a new relationship or establishing a sense of reconnection. Have you ever met up with a friend you've not seen in a long time and found conversation tricky to jump into? The easiest way to reconnect is by diving into a juicy, wonderful memory you both share. Let's look at other ways sharing a story from your past can be used to strengthen relationships.

Building trust

Sharing personal stories from your past can foster trust because it allows others to see you in the moment, including your flaws and past mistakes. This understanding builds genuine and lasting connections in relationships and fosters a sense of trust between both parties because of what is shared. An example of how sharing a story from your past can build trust in the relationship can be seen in the popular 2012 movie, *Silver Linings Playbook*. Pat is a man recently released from a mental institution trying to rebuild his life. He soon develops a friendship with Tiffany, who is also dealing with emotional struggles. In a pivotal scene, Pat and Tiffany sit down together to share their personal stories and open up about their past, struggles and experiences. This exchange allows them to understand each other's pain and vulnerabilities, and fosters a strong bond and trust between the two. It's because of this level of openness, that that they lay the foundation for a trusting relationship and strong connection.

Real-life application: Opening up with your new friend/partner about a difficult experience from your past

Here are five tips on how to make space for a story from your past when you want to be open with a new friend or partner.

1. **Setting**

    Choose the right time and place for your focused conversation. Typically, this will be somewhere both of you have time to share without any interruptions. Make sure you're both relaxed and receptive, and that the medium of storytelling is correct for whatever is being shared. For example, you won't want to send anything via text that would be better explained face-to-face.

2. **Gentle introduction**

    Begin by letting them know that you'd like share something significant from your past because you trust them with the information. Emphasise that while it can be difficult for you to share this, having them be aware of it will be beneficial for your relationship and help them understand you better. This will help assist your friend/partner in preparing themselves emotionally for what you're going to share.

3. **Boundaries**

    Be clear about your boundaries before you share. Let them know what they can do with the information (e.g. can they share it with other people?), and let them know how you'd like them to listen. Perhaps you want to talk and get the whole story out there before they say anything? If so, communicate this boundary clearly at the start and ask for their support and understanding. This will help establish this trust between the two of you.

4. **Express yourself authentically**

    The more open and honest you are about your emotions and thoughts regarding this story, the more your friend/partner will connect to you. Share how the experience impacted you and any vulnerabilities it may have created in you.

5. **Deepen trust**

    Following the conversation, deepen the trust by opening the floor up to your partner and encouraging them to ask questions, express their feelings or share their thoughts.

This two-way dialogue will demonstrate that you also value their thoughts and emotions, and perhaps they will open up and share something with you.

SELF

By reflecting on our stories, we can gain clarity on our emotions and understand our reactions to certain situations. This helps us become more self-aware and develop strategies for managing our emotions in the future.

Increased self-awareness

Oprah Winfrey has been a talk-show host, actress, producer, media executive and philanthropist. With so many titles under her belt, she certainly has a lot of narratives to make space for, and she discussed the significance of doing this her own life in her book *What Happened To You?: Conversations on Trauma, Resilience, and Healing*.

Looking back on her life's journey and all the challenges she'd faced assisted her in developing a deep sense of self and understanding. She said, 'Your past is not an excuse. But it is an explanation offering insight into the questions so many of us ask ourselves: Why do I behave the way I behave? Why do I feel the way I do?'.[2] This is exactly what step one is about. By acknowledging the value of past narratives and understanding that reflecting on them provides insight, Oprah emphasises the role that introspection plays in a greater sense of self-awareness. Only by looking back on your story will you develop a greater understanding of who you are.

Real-life application: Journaling to assist you in making a big decision

Here are five tips on how to reflect on your past narratives and use those insights to help you make a decision.

1. **Assess your past**

    Look back on your narratives and gauge if you've had a similar situation or decision to make in the past. Evaluate the outcomes from those (both positive and negative) and consider what worked well and what was not so great.

2. **Identify recurring patterns**

    See if you can spot a recurring theme or pattern in your decision-making process. Reflect on all you've learned in step one and ask yourself if perhaps you've been living a particular story for a reason. This will allow you the chance to make a conscious effort to break any negative patterns or reinforce positive ones.

3. **Reflect on your values**

    Consider past narratives that left you feeling content, proud or fulfilled and why that was the case. See if you can identify which choice would align with those positive stories you've already experienced.

4. **Practice self-compassion**

    Be kind to yourself! Give yourself a pat on the back for how much you've grown and learned along the way. Consider how that wisdom can be applied to help you feel empowered as you make this next decision.

5. **Tune in to self**

    While it's important to seek advice from trusted friends, family or mentors, it's important to know that you have the full picture. Take a moment to really listen to what your heart is telling you it wants, and then give yourself the space to hear it.

CHAPTER FOUR

Step 2: Knowing who you (truly) are

'Knowing yourself is the beginning of all wisdom.'
Aristotle, *Greek Philosopher*

The most significant discovery in life is unveiling who you are and standing in that truth. Yet, following those sweet cookie crumbs to self-realisation can be tricky. Some people will actively decide the journey is too hard, so they'll forgo it altogether – turning up the volume in other areas of their life so they can drown out the desires of their heart. Maybe they're fearful of confronting their truth or terrified they won't have the strength to live by it, but by avoiding this journey entirely, they fail to connect to their inner truth and lack the self-awareness needed for productive internal investigation.

A person who is disconnected from their true self is more vulnerable to listening to the lies their inner critic feeds them or, worse, adopting a plot that isn't their own. This might be driven by some of those influential elements we discussed in chapter one, or because they've never asked themselves the big questions like 'Who am I?' and 'What is it that I truly want for my life?' Whatever the reason for living a plot that isn't theirs, the song and dance of pretending to be something you're not is exhausting and unsustainable.

When I first started doing this work, 'Who are you?' was one of the first questions I asked every new client. Usually, the person answering would go into robot mode without drawing a breath and give me a generic response. My clients – let's call her Courtney – answer was no different: 'I'm a mum, a fifth-grade teacher and a wife'. The long pause that followed signified that she was ready for my next question. That's who she thought she was. End of story.

I circled back and gently pressed her again. 'Who is Courtney in those roles?' Her face softened. 'Well,' she answered slowly. 'I teach, and I take care of my family . . .' The way she spoke made it sound as if she were asking me a question – trying to gauge if her answer was correct.

'Okay,' I nodded. 'But who are *you*?'

There was silence again, and it was very telling. Courtney didn't know the answer. As we continued talking, I discovered this question was one she had never asked herself. She admitted to feeling that people who asked that type of question were either 'wrapped up in themselves' or 'selfish'. Somewhere in her past, she'd confused self-understanding with self-indulgence. By the end of our session, we'd separated these two concepts from each other, giving Courtney the ability to reconnect with who she was at her core.

In my experience, Courtney is far from the only person who views the idea of 'finding yourself' as a luxurious endeavour or an inherently self-centred quest. This misconception is widespread and incorrect. In fact, the opposite is true: investigating this very human question and confirming the answer is actually an *unselfish* process because knowing who are connects you to the root of every story you interact with in life – yours and other people's. And when you show up as the true version of yourself in parenting, friendships, relationships, and work environments, your personal journey of self-reflection benefits the collective in so many ways.

In order to be the most valuable version of yourself and live in alignment with the narratives that are destined for you, it's imperative to know who you are, what you value and what you have to offer. This degree of self-knowledge is not always easy to achieve, especially when someone has been forced to fit into a specific box their whole life. Continuous pressure to live a certain way and fit a mould others have made for us pulls us further away from the person we really are inside.

The benefits of persevering with this quest for truth is well worth the effort, however. Exploring the true self is where an individual's real story begins because understanding who you are makes you more self-aware, and this newfound awareness means you can better understand not only your own thoughts, emotions and behaviours, but also how they impact others. Suddenly, your confidence picks up when making decisions or showcasing your abilities because now you know exactly what your strengths and weaknesses are. You might feel a newly found sense of clarity around your goals and an increased focus on priorities that funnel into a larger feeling of purpose.

It's no surprise that relationships tend to improve as a result of this self-reflection. You can communicate more honestly and effectively and set boundaries that align with your values, all while taking better care of yourself. With better boundaries, your mental, psychical and emotional health improves as you make choices supporting your well-being. Heck, you've never felt more alive!

All the while, you are growing and identifying new areas to work on as you take steps to become the best version of yourself. All of these improvements combine to enhance your storytelling powers, and this chapter is designed to show you how. To dive into this step, we will unpack the role of the true self within storytelling and start to map out what that looks like for you. We'll explore who you are at your core, and investigate how you can remain connected to your most authentic self throughout your life.

The role of the 'true self' in story

The term 'true self' often gets a bad rap, as does its sister term, 'authentic'. A mention of one of these words in a conversation might cause the listener's eyes to roll to the back of their heads, but every now and again, you'll find someone else who 'gets it'. Often, that someone has also done the work, understands its value and is already implementing its power into their expression of self through their storytelling. Knowing who you are, can make you a better storyteller simply because you are speaking from a place of clarity. When you are rooted in your values, beliefs and motivations, you move accordingly in a clear, focused and impactful direction regardless of any chaos or indecision around you.

Knowledge of self helps you to tell stories that reflect your real experience and speak your truth. This type of authenticity is crucial if you want to engage with an audience because people are not stupid. They can spot a disingenuous story from a mile away. Engaging in stories that are not your own does a disservice to you, and your audience. It's only when you can be honest about your experiences that your storytelling becomes relatable and impactful.

***

When I was pregnant, I was uncomfortable as hell. My body was changing, and while I desperately wanted to be one of those goddess-like mamas-to-be, I was more of the legging-wearing, heat-pack on me 24/7, groaning kinda gals. I'd scroll Instagram reading as much as I could about what was happening to my body and mind (not a good idea, btw), and time and time again, I'd be shown carefully curated accounts from women who shared *nothing* about the challenging parts of pregnancy and only the picture-perfect moments. That is, until I stumbled across a post from Amy Gerard. What a breath of fresh air!

As I scrolled through Amy's feed, I felt an instant connection and rush of relief. *Oh, thank God!* I thought. *Someone else feels the same.* Her posts revealed every spick and speck of truth about her experience of being pregnant and raising small children: the good, the bad and the ugly. She expressed herself with such humour and honesty that I could feel her authenticity from the other side of the world. There was no 'pretty filler'. It was just her truth, and she was just herself.

Many years later, Amy and I connected on my podcast, where she shared how important it was for her to remain true to her values while sharing her life. She understands that what connects others to her experience of motherhood is her authentic expression of it. As her brand and business continue to grow, she sticks to her guns and remains the same Amy she's been from the very start.

You might be wondering how you can start to reconnect with your true self. First, you must define what 'true self' means to you. I believe it's the most genuine and authentic aspect of us. Who we are at our core. To help illustrate the difference between the physical self and the true self, I like to break the concept of 'self' into three main parts:

1. **The body and mind self:** This is the identity and ego – the part of us that identifies as being an individual being in a human body. It can become trapped by labels and perform for other people, as we've explored.

2. **The true self or 'soul layer':** This is the spiritual essence of us, which cannot be contained within a body. It connects us with our truth. It's who we feel we are in our heart of hearts.

3. **The universe, nature, source, or God (whatever you resonate with):** This is the essence that connects everything and everyone.

A part of reconnecting with your true self involves connecting to what is in your heart and soul. Reconnecting can look a little different for each person. Some find their true self instantly, while others can get a little lost. To explain why this might be, let me introduce the true self types I've observed through my work.

1. The 'just-around-the-corner' true self

You know exactly where your true self is located, and you can find your way home to it. Every now and again, you might wander a little too far, turn a corner and realise you're nowhere near where you should be. But you never stress because you know how to take a breath, reconnect and get home.

2. The 'crossroads' true self

You tend to get distracted easily and don't always pay attention to where you're going. Sometimes, you look up to find you've reached a crossroads. There's street A or street B, but neither option feels familiar or right. What's worse, you have no freaking idea how to get back to your true self. So, you take a guess and hope it's the right one. Street B it is! (Or was it A?)

3. The 'in the dark' true self

You've also been distracted and not paying attention to your path. Now the streetlights are off and it's dark. You're panicking because you can't read the signs to find your way home. (Where is home again?) You're paralysed. Terrified to move in any direction in case it's the wrong one. Instead, you remain there – silent. Hoping someone will come to your rescue.

Don't panic if number three sounds like your present situation. In this chapter, we will dig down to find out who your true self is, so you can reconnect to that sense of self again, find your way home, and tell better stories because of it. By the end of this step, you'll understand why it's best to connect to yourself frequently. To help you do this, I suggest incorporating one of more of the strategies listed in your routine.

Spend time alone: One of best ways to reconnect with ourselves is to spend time alone, yet many of us hardly ever do this! If you do, use this time to reflect on your thoughts and feelings and to get in touch with your inner self.

Practice mindfulness: Mindfulness involves paying attention to the present moment without judgement. I do this through meditation. This can help us become more aware of our thoughts and feelings and nurture a deeper understanding of ourselves.

Write in a journal: Journaling can be a powerful way to connect with ourselves because it slows us down, allowing us to explore thoughts and feelings more deeply, set goals and intentions, and track our progresses over the short and long term.

Engage in creative activities: Creative activities including painting, drawing, writing or playing music help us express ourselves in new and different ways. Tapping into our inner creativity can do some special things for the self, including engaging different parts of the brain and allowing us to connect to our emotions and thoughts without always using words.

Practice self-care: This one might seem obvious, but taking care of ourselves is integral to reconnecting with our true self. Getting enough sleep, eating well, exercising, and practising relaxation techniques like yoga are all great ways of doing this.

Take a break from technology: It can be a useful tool, but it also distract us from our inner selves. Taking a break from tech helps us disconnect from the outside world and connect more deeply within.

Connect with nature: This is such a powerful way to reconnect with ourselves. Whether you go for a walk in the bush, sit by a lake, or hang out in a backyard, being in nature can help us feel more grounded and connected to the world around us.

Reconnect with the passions of your inner child

Each one of us has something that we are naturally drawn to; an activity, concept or topic we can completely lose ourselves in. If we follow these passions, dreams and commitments, they can ignite our souls and help us lead purposeful lives. It's a common perception that as life unfolds, we find insights along the way that lead us to our path, but I believe we're aware of them from a much younger age. When we're young, we know more about ourselves than we're given credit for. If you reflect on what lit you up as a child and what you instinctually felt was interesting, fun or important, you can collect powerful insights about yourself.

As a child, I loved to read. One of my earliest memories is of my mum reading me one of those books that plays phrases when you press a button. I was three, and after we'd read this book for the hundredth time, I asked Mum if she thought I'd be able to read it by myself one day. I so desperately wanted to read and command the book on my own. She laughed and said, 'Of course, Sweetie. When you go to school.' Learn to read I did, and my love for books and reading grew with me.

Instinctually, I knew even then that I loved storytelling, and I'm so glad I never lost that passion. We can lose our natural childhood wonder when we are conditioned or told that our interests are not practical, worthy or realistic. Perhaps you always knew what you loved but were never given a chance to explore it or participate in that thing your small heart desired. The good news is, you're grown now! And those childhood pleasures – whether you explored them in childhood or not – can still open a door in your adult life. The child you were is still inside you somewhere, harbouring the same desires, and hopes it did decades ago. This is the perfect time to connect with that child and find what out what's inside its heart.

Storyteller session 5:
Listen to your inner child

Think of what you used to love and try to remember the inner nudges and pulls you experienced in your younger years. Answer the below questions to gain insight into the things you were naturally drawn to:

1. What did I want to be when I was older?
2. Did I become that thing? If not, why?
3. What topics was I curious about when I was younger?
4. What was my favourite subject in school? Why?
5. What did I spend my time dreaming about?
6. Which aspects of my childhood brought me the most happiness and joy? Do I still integrate those aspects into my adult life? Why/Why not?

Chances are, many of the answers you provided are still things you're naturally drawn to. Give yourself permission to explore them again. If surfing was your thing back then, get back in the water. If you loved art, go pick up a new sketchpad and see if that spark is still here.

A make-up bag for the soul

If you're anything like me, you have a lot of makeup and no clue how to use most of it, so you keep it in one place to keep it tidy and off the bathroom counter. Enter the makeup bag. The bag I'm proposing here, though, is a little different because it's a metaphorical one, designed to house the multiple parts of your true self that combine to make you, you. To house all of these, you need a neat, organised make-up bag (i.e. your body). There are six compartments in this bag, and each one holds an item that represents an aspect of the true you.

1. Passions

Passions are best described as intense feelings, interests or pursuits that compel us to engage in certain hobbies, goals or activities. These are the motivations that make us willing to invest incredible amounts of time, energy and resources into achieving or experiencing something, so they play a significant role in shaping our lives. A hobby, career aspiration, relationship, creative endeavour or social cause that we are passionate about can add a sense of purpose, fulfilment and satisfaction to life. Passions can even drive us to overcome challenges or setbacks and continue to achieve our goals.

Identifying passions is essential on the journey to discover the true self because these are likely to be the things that make you feel the most alive. A clue to identifying them is to see what gets your heart racing. Take note of moments when you feel energised, inspired and excited because that's how it feels when you're participating in something that is passion-worthy to you.

Storyteller session 6:
Rekindling old passions

Answer the below questions to provide insight into your passions might be.

1. Reflect on your experiences as an adult to date. Which activities or experiences have brought you the most joy, fulfilment or sense of desire?

2. Write a list of the things you already know bring a sense of passion to your life.
   - Do any of these pursuits link with the answers you gave in the previous question or share a common goal/outcome?

3. Can you think of a time a passion strengthened your storytelling? Why do you think that was? (Don't worry if you aren't sure. I'll tell you at the end of the chapter!)

2. Talents

All of us have unique talents, and understanding what yours are will help you feel more at home within your true self. Talent doesn't mean you do something perfectly, it simply means there are certain things you are naturally more gifted at than other people. It's important to be aware of these talents so you can use them to aide your storytelling.

Your talents are the things that help you to stand out, achieve success and move through life. Buying or faking a talent is not usually possible. To access a talent and tap into its power, you really have to be connected to your true self. An example of this is playing the guitar. You cannot fake this skill or buy that talent, and even if you spend forever practising, you will likely never be as good as someone who is naturally gifted player. That's okay! In our digital age, it's easy to compare one person's natural talent with that of another. Still, it can be a little trickier to spot natural talent in ourselves, especially if we're not open to letting our true self be seen or okay with what that looks like in its entirety.

I'm hopeful that by this stage in the book, you understand how crucial being the real you is to tapping into your storytelling power. Being the real you includes embracing your natural talents, no matter how insignificant you might think they are. While I've already given you the guitar example, it's worth mentioning that talents are extremely diverse as well as large and small scale. You might be talented at making people feel welcome, giving advice or even styling an outfit. Don't discount these smaller-scale talents because they are hugely valuable, too.

Storyteller session 7:
What are your talents?

What things are you naturally good at doing? Answer the below questions to provide insight into your talents.

1. What do people often tell you you're good at?
2. What can you do faster than others?
3. What do you find easy that others find difficult?
4. Write a list of what you believe your top three talents are. Why did you select these three in particular?

3. Skills

I've placed this item directly under talents because, while related, people often get skills and talents confused. Talents are natural gifts while skills are acquired through learning, practice and dedication. Like talents, skills can also help you stand out, achieve success and move through life, but honing a skill requires effort and time on your part. Understanding this difference can help you take some pressure off yourself because it allows you to separate the things you've learned to be good at from the stuff you're naturally good at.

Sometimes, a skill we acquire might compliment or enhance a natural talent, which is terrific! Either way, it is important to identify your strengths and weaknesses to identify areas that can be improved or developed further. Sometimes, all it takes is the right teacher.

Storyteller session 8:
What skills have you acquired?

Answer the questions below to gain insights into the skills you've already built.

1. What have you learned that you are now an expert in?
2. Is there something you've continued practising that you've become fantastic at?
3. Which skills would you list on a resumé?
4. Did a teacher or someone in your life help you gain the skills you needed to move forward on your path?

4. Gifts

No, I'm not talking about your love language or a present for your birthday. Gifts are the parts of your soul that shine through you. I describe these as our best qualities and call them gifts because, often, we share them with others in the form of acts of service or love. Gifts are the positive attributes that you possess at your core.

Storyteller session 9:
Which gifts will you share?

Here are a few words that describe gifts someone might possess. Take your time to look over them, then circle any you feel you naturally have and share with others. Perhaps others have told you that you possess a certain gift. Make a note of any you have and add additional gifts you resonate with.

Entertaining	Supportive	Kind
Gentle	Adventurous	Courageous
Knowledgeable	Patient	Practical
Encouraging	Funny	Strong
Open	Quick-witted	Calm
Inspiring	Reliable	Flexible

5: Weaknesses

True self includes the word 'true' for a reason: it wouldn't be true if it were all rosy. Our true self includes our weaknesses, and those are best described as qualities and traits that hinder us from reaching our potential or performing in a desired way. Everyone has them, and they can be related to many things, such as our skills, knowledge, habits, attitudes and behaviours. Confronting our weaknesses and looking at them with compassion allows us to identify areas we need to improve in.

It's important to note that weaknesses are not inherently negative or terrible. Embracing them is simply another step to knowing the true self. There's no point dwelling on them or being a sook about them. Call it like you see it and own up to the things you aren't the best at. Doing this will help you move in the right direction.

Storyteller session 10:
Confronting your weaknesses

It's time to talk about the not-so-fun stuff, but I promise it's worth it. Answer the below questions to gain insight into your weaknesses.

1. What things are you not-so-great at?
2. Are there things you really don't enjoy doing? What are they? Do you identify any of these as weaknesses of yours?
3. List the things you struggle with most and consider why they don't come easy to you. Are any of them similar in nature?

6: Values
We're up to the last item in the make-up bag, and this one should be the easiest to tackle because values are the guiding principles, ideals

and beliefs that influence your attitudes, decisions and behaviours in day-to-day life. Your values provide a sort of map that guides your interactions in personal, social and professional settings, but not all of them necessarily reflect your true self. As we discussed when we talked about conditioning, many factors shape our values. The key is to identify which values resonate with the true self. To do that, you need to ask a big question: what do I stand for? Be open to this answer changing over time since values can evolve as you grow and experience new things.

Storyteller session 11:
What are your true values?

Here are some questions to help you examine your values. Take your time answering these questions and really allow yourself the space to sit with the answers.

1. What is important to you in life?
2. What do you stand for?
3. What qualities do you pride yourself on?
4. What are your non-negotiables in relationships and friendships?
5. What things are you are willing to fight for or defend?
6. What qualities do you admire in others? Why?

Do any of your answers surprise you? Likely not. This is because you already know all of the answers at your core. They reflect the truest version of you.

This is a lot of self-reflection, I know. But it's important to reconnect with the items in this make-up bag of the soul, because when life gets busy and complicated, it's easy to forget these parts of ourselves and replace them with items that are not our shade. We put those new items in and then rush through life thinking we look pretty natural, meanwhile everyone can see that we've got the wrong colours on! It's not until we take a close look in the mirror that we realise we've been walking around looking like an imposter. The stories we tell are deeply affected by our ability or inability to reflect our true selves to our listeners, and even ourselves.

Applying step 2 in real life

With step two, you've gained even greater insight into your true self and how to use it to build a foundation so you can become a more compelling storyteller. Let's examine how being authentically yourself can improve your storytelling in real life.

WORK

One day, my friend and I were debating the benefits of being yourself at work. Her position was that bringing your personal self to the workplace was a no-no. She argued that when you're at work, you're expected to be professional. I disagreed because I believe it's possible to be professional, yet still reflect your true self. In fact, I think depending on your profession or industry, being yourself can really assist your success in your career or business.

I believe that bringing your knowledge, passions, values, talents and skills, not to mention awareness of your weaknesses, to work can make you a much better employee or business owner. Rather than ignoring those aspects of yourself and putting on a robotic-like facade, you'll be able to integrate the things that are most important to you into what you do for a living, which is how most of us spend the majority of our time.

The following helps showcase how knowing your true self and integrating that into your professional life can elevate your storytelling on the job.

Building brand connection

Businesses that effectively communicate their point of difference by knowing and embracing their true, unique identity are able to build a connection between the brand and its consumers. Outdoor clothing and gear company, Patagonia is a great example of this because in spite of industry trends, they have remained consistent to who they are and what they stand for. The brand is built around their mission to 'build the best product, cause no unnecessary harm, and use business to inspire and implement solutions to the environmental crisis'. Meeting these aims is no small feat in a world of fast fashion, cheap manufacturing and capitalism. To achieve this ambitious mission, Patagonia focuses on environmental activism by actively participating in campaigns and donating a portion of profits to educating their customers about the environmental impact of fashion and talking about how their supply chain differs to their competitors. They also promote buying less by investing in high-quality items that last longer to avoid waste, and promote fair labor practices with safe and ethical working conditions. By staying true to their brand's purpose and mission, and effectively communicating the company values and points of difference though marketing campaigns and brand advertising they have cultivated a loyal customer base who appreciate and align with their unique identity.

Real-life application: Communicate your point of difference in your personal business

Here are five tips on how to share a brand message with a target audience.

1. **Define your unique value proposition**

   Start by identifying what sets this particular brand apart from competitors in the same industry. Clearly define what value the brand offers to the customer/client, and be as specific as possible. Perhaps it's a superior quality, better service or particular beliefs.

2. **Create a messaging plan**

   Create a clear and concise messaging plan that is tailored to the brand and craft all communication in a way that expresses the true essence of the brand. Use language, tone, and messaging to highlight what makes this brand unique and be clear when sharing the story of how various initiatives, products or services reflect the true ethos, mission and vision for the business.

3. **Use consistent branding**

    Establish a strong visual identity with the use of branding elements such as logos, colours, fonts or imagery across all of your communication channels. Websites, social media handles, marketing materials and other customer interactions with branding must remain consistent in tone and visual identity to increase its familiarity with the target audience.

4. **Provide proof**

    Showcase that the brand is who you say it is when it comes to business and point of difference. You can do this by providing case studies, customer testimonials, certifications, involvement or any other form of validation required for your industry that reflect what the brand is truly all about.

5. **Service/create for your market**

    Actively seek out the customer/client base who is already aligned with the brand's values and mission so they can support it. Listen to their specific feedback and then service them appropriately by demonstrating how much you value their input and loyalty.

RELATIONSHIPS

Expressing who we are at our core benefits relationships at any stage of their lifecycle. This is because knowing yourself and sharing through that lens is necessary for building healthy and fulfilling relationships, be that with colleagues, friends, family or romantic partners. As you express the truth of what you think and feel, the people in your life will come to know you so much better.

Self-knowledge can also help you to navigate the ups and downs that all relationships go through because you'll be able to anchor yourself. Another benefit is that being yourself will protect your energy, because let's face it, it's exhausting to keep up appearances or behave in an inauthentic way. Here are a few ways that knowing your true self can be applied to storytelling in the context of relationships.

Successful dating

Imagine a person named Joy who is an adventurous and outdoorsy kinda girl. She is passionate about hiking, camping and exploring new places, and is now interested in finding a romantic partner. At a local networking event for singles who want to mingle, Joy is thrilled to find the room filled with so many potential suitors (what a great turn out!). She works the floor with one rule in mind, *Be your true self.*

Before leaving the house this evening, Joy set herself this rule so she would be nothing but her true self, and communicate her real nature and passions. She knows that this will give her a better chance of connecting with someone on an authentic level. Joy is not here to waste time – she's got adventures to have! After interacting with a few men who look visibly bored (and even scared) of her stories of outdoor adventuring, she moves on. Then, she meets Dave.

When she shares stories about her favourite hiking trails and camping trips, Dave is eager to see photos before he whips out his phone to show her his own. They spend the next hour connecting over their active lifestyles and upcoming quests. They exchange numbers with the intention of going on one of these adventures together, and this leads to a successful date a few weeks later. Joy's decision to communicate her true nature as an adventurous outdoorsy person attracted a partner who was interested in joining her and because of that, she created a dating experience that aligned with her authentic self and eventually created a successful relationship with Dave.

Real-life application: Create a dating profile that communicates who you (truly) are

Here are five tips on how to share who you truly are on your online dating profiles.

1. **Be honest**

    Authenticity is key when it comes to online dating. As Joy's story illustrates, presenting yourself accurately and honestly in a way that highlights your real interests, hobbies and values will bring you closer to attracting someone who is genuinely interested in you.

2. **Showcase your personality**

    Sharing stories, experiences and anecdotes can reveal your spirit. Whether that be through expressing humor, kindness or in another unique way, it will help convey your sense of character and personality so potential suitors can connect with your profile and get in touch.

3. **Be specific**

    The more specific you can be in these profiles, the better!

Being specific about certain details makes it easier for like-minded individuals to find common ground with you. Instead of saying 'I like to food,' say, 'I like Italian food. Pesto prawn linguini is my favourite.'

4. **Include clear and recent photos**
   Being who you truly are involves being comfortable with what you look like. Include clear photos that capture the real you and avoid any photoshopping or catfishing tricks (I'm sure you wouldn't do that!).

5. **Avoid clichés**
   Stay clear of clichés such as 'likes longs walks on the beach' to ensure you don't blend in with the crowd. Instead, focus on expressing the true you to make your profile more memorable.

SELF

Understanding ourselves at our core is crucial for personal growth because knowing who we are and embracing our true selves allows us to make informed decisions, set meaningful goals, and pursue a path aligned with our true values. By understanding our strengths, weaknesses, and more, we can focus our energy on activities and pursuits that bring us joy and fulfillment and feel confident in doing so.

Improving self-confidence

Actor Viola Davis is world famous for her award-winning performances in films and TV shows, but what makes her stand out in my mind is how open she's been about sharing her personal journey with confidence, and how understanding her true self has helped her build self-confidence. In various interviews and in her memoir, *Finding Me*, Viola speaks about how her challenging upbringing – clouded with poverty and racism – meant she struggled to feel worthy and visible.

Despite this, Viola embarked on an acting career and found that embracing her authentic self, with all its flaws, allowed her to tap into a greater level of connection to her characters and bring a remarkable truthfulness to them. Acknowledging her true self gave her a greater sense of self-confidence – one that inspires others to embrace their own uniqueness and find confidence in their true selves. Viola's story highlights the transformative power of self-acceptance and shows that by understanding and embracing who we really are, we can improve our self-confidence.

Real-life application: Looking in the mirror and feeling more confident with who you see

Here are five tips on how reflecting and acknowledging who you truly are can make you feel more confident.

1. **Positive self-talk**

    Be mindful of the thoughts you're having when you first look in the mirror. Replace self-critical thoughts with self-compassion and positive ones. Remind yourself of your strengths, achievements and the qualities you most admire or appreciate about yourself. Repeat those thoughts to yourself out loud to reinforce them.

2. **Embrace your favourite parts**

    True beauty comes from within and is not determined

by external appearances. With that said, what are your favourite parts about yourself that are not on your physical body? Are you kind, funny, efficient? Remind yourself of your favourite parts and celebrate them often.

3. **Avoid comparison**

   Resist the urge to compare yourself. Be that to a version of yourself from 10 years ago or to another person. Stand in the truth of who you are today and own it. You are on your own unique journey, so acknowledge this by saying it out loud.

4. **Celebrate your body**

   Which of your body parts do you love? What part of you physically helps you feel like you? Your hair? Your eyes? Your smile? Your ability to be mobile? Celebrate the parts of your body you're grateful for.

5. **Be kind**

   Most importantly, boost your confidence by simply being kind to yourself. Practice self-compassion and be patient with yourself. Building self-confidence takes time and practice and that it's okay for it to not feel natural the first few times.

CHAPTER FIVE

Step 3: Crafting a strong purpose

> 'Once you begin the journey toward a life of purpose, you enter the realm of real magic.'
> **Dr Wayne Dyer**, *Real Magic*

I love reality television. It's a guilty pleasure. And though I know it's not exactly 'high art', I've been sucked into the Bravo Universe ever since I watched my first episode of *The Real Housewives of Beverly Hills*. This love affair has evolved and spread beyond the Bravo network to the streaming giants and their endless options of ready-to-watch randoms. If there is a niche or interest out there, there is probably a reality television show about it.

If I were to conjure up the reality show of my dreams, here's how I would pitch it: 'Twenty complete strangers who all feel lost in their current lives enter the house for a four-week transformational journey. Armed with nothing but their hearts, stories and soul, and using only therapeutic practices and self-evaluations, they will connect to their deepest desires and identify their 'why'. The prize? Purpose and direction.'

Now *that* pitch gets me going, but something tells me networks wouldn't jump to pick it up it. Trust me, though, this niche exists. So many of us can relate to feeling a sense of anxiety when words like 'purpose' and 'direction' get thrown around, and that's usually because we're struggling to identify our own. You betcha people would tune in to see what those housemates found out!

Purpose gives you direction in life from which you can derive meaning. It motivates, inspires and guides us through life as we make decisions and face life's inevitable challenges, and is significant at every stage of our lives. We draw on it for our physical, mental and emotional wellbeing.

Psychologists Edward Deci and Richard Ryan developed a theory called the Self-Determination Theory (or SDT) around the framework of human motivation and personality development. This theory suggests that having a sense of direction and purpose in life is necessary for psychological well-being, and that three essential needs have to be met in order to achieve this well-being.

> **Autonomy:** The need to feel control/direction over one's life.
> **Competence:** The need to feel capable of actioning one's life.
> **Relatedness:** The need to connect to others through one's life.[3]

When these needs are met, we're more likely to feel satisfied with our life and a sense of purpose, leading to a better overall outcome. When the opposite occurs, and we feel dissatisfied or disconnected from these needs, we're more likely to experience distress and disengagement.

I truly believe that our audience experiences a similar disengagement when the stories we tell lack purpose. If you learned about story structure back in school, you may have learned that a 'main direction' is vital to a story's success because this is the thing that ensures a clear and concise focus. The core purpose of a story creates a structured plot and coherent theme that ties the story together.

As a (rather drastic) example, say we're telling a story about a girl named Leah in a post-apocalyptic world. She embarks on a dangerous journey to find clean water for her family, and along the way she faces challenges and meets other survivors who either help or hinder her mission. Throughout her quest she learns about resilience, hardship and sacrifice, while retaining her core purpose of seeking water to save her family. It's Leah's core purpose that gives her story direction. If a core purpose is absent from a story, the audience will be confused, dissatisfied and disengage.

A clear purpose anchors our story and gives it a strong core that helps us avoid crafting aimless narratives. It also channels our focus to help us achieve our goals and connect to others in an impactful way. If we apply SDT's approach to storytelling, we could say that in order to have strong stories, three essential needs must be fulfilled.

Autonomy: The need to feel control/direction over one's story.
Competence: The need to feel capable of sharing one's story.
Relatedness: The need to connect to others through one's story.

As we work through this third step of our storytelling journey, we'll explore how crafting a strong purpose within ourselves increases our power and helps us achieve a desired outcome when we share our voice.

Getting anchored in your 'priority purpose'

Have you ever made a vision board? As soon as I finished reading *The Secret* by Rhonda Byrne, I busted out the scissors and glue. *You mean I can have a JEEP Wrangler if I stick a picture of one on a board and then visualise myself owning one?* I'd been inspired by Byrne's description of the Law of Attraction, which states that everything in the universe is made up of energy and has a vibrational frequency. According to this law. people can attract both positive or negative experiences into their lives through the power of their thoughts and feelings. To put it plainly, if you focus your thoughts and emotions on positive outcomes, it will likely attract those positive things to you, and vice versa. There are finer details and more specifics to the Law of Attraction is a discussion for another day, but what I want to bring your attention to are the beliefs you hold around the items you choose to place on that vision board.

When dreaming up an 'ideal' life, a lot of people tend to fill these boards with images of material things like cars, houses or vacations, believing those things will give them a sense of purpose or direction in life – like arrows pointing to a target that spells success with a capital S. However, if we were to obtain these things in real life, they might provide feelings of accomplishment and meaning, but only temporarily. They won't satisfy our internal hunger for purpose. And if we're not anchored to our core, soon enough, we'll be left wanting more. This is why some of the wealthiest people report a lack of fulfilment and direction – they are not anchored in their purpose. This may also explain why, conversely, others living much simpler, modest lives might be happier if they are connected to their why.

So, what is this magical P word all about? Purpose is the overarching force driving your life – it's sometimes referred to as a person's 'north star' because it can be used to help them navigate thoughts, decisions , behaviour and (yep, you guessed it) even their stories. Purpose connects you to a more profound sense of meaning and satisfaction in life because it aligns with your true self and goes beyond external material factors. Without purpose driving and showing up in every story you express, you are missing out on a key piece of your power.

A common misconception is that each of us only has one purpose for our whole life. I don't subscribe to that. I believe we can have multiple purposes throughout our lives because purpose will change and evolve with us. This is why it's important to check in with yourself and evaluate something I like to call your 'priority purpose'. This is the purpose driving your current story – the one that matters in this particular chapter of your life. Whenever you share a story, it should be anchored in this core, i.e., your priority purpose.

Typically, there will be a common thread linking all of your purposes together, and often, that thread might simply reflect the stage of life you are in. If your purpose has always been caring for and helping your loved ones, as you move through life this might shift from caring for your younger siblings to parenting your own child. In mid-life, it might become caring for your elderly parents, and so on. Every decision, expression and move you make is likely made with your current purpose in front of your mind. If it's not, then we need to get started on reconnecting you to yours today!

Storyteller session 12:
What is your priority purpose?

- What brings you joy and lights you up?
- What are you willing to struggle, work or fight for?
- What impact do you want to have on the world?
- What do you want to dedicate yourself to? Why?
- What do you see as your duty or calling?
- What will you stop at nothing to achieve? Why?

Answering these questions can help you spot your purpose by shining a light on what brings you a sense of fulfilment. These insights help point you towards a path that aligns with things that hold deep significance to you. Take the opportunity to review your answers. Do any common themes emerge? Is there a thread that linking the things you care most about? Take time to get curious about this.

Getting clear on your purpose and being aware of its influence on your life can help you take practical steps to better align with it no matter your current circumstance. When I interviewed author and entrepreneur Mariam Elhouli about her inspiring journey, she told me she'd had a greater vision beyond work in the forefront of her mind, anchoring her to her purpose and pulling her forward. After experiencing the horrors of war in Lebanon while a mother herself, her purpose became clear as day: to provide a better life for her family.

Family became Mariam's north star as she worked on returning home to the safety of Australia, finishing her education and following her passions. Every interaction and decision was made with her family's welfare front of mind. Today, Mariam's name is on billboards in New York City and she writes books she hopes will help readers understand other perspectives and believe in themselves, even when nobody else does. Your purpose is the thing that gives you permission to make changes and move in your desired direction.

What's holding you back?

Sometimes, the thing keeping us from moving in our desired direction is ourselves – often for reasons we don't even understand. When this happens, we must discover what stops us from integrating that core – that priority purpose – into our daily actions. You can know exactly where you've come from, who you are and what you are here to do, but still feel like something is holding you back from expressing all of these things. Whether it's an inability to speak your mind or share your passions, you feel frozen and unable to communicate the purpose burning inside of you.

Often, fear is the thing holding you back. Getting anchored in your purpose is the best way to overcome this fear. Unmoored, you are more likely to struggle with self-doubt and uncertainty, or have a sense of insecurity sweep in. You might lack the conviction to connect with your message, which is essential for any storyteller. Here are the four main fears people commonly struggle with.

1. **Fear of judgement:** This manifests as an intense fear about the negative opinions of others. When we are afraid of being negatively evaluated, criticised, laughed at or even looked down on by others, it can stop us from behaving the way we want to avoid embarrassment or humiliation.
   Statement: *I won't follow my dreams because I'm afraid of what people will say.*

2. **Fear of conflict:** Being unable to speak your mind and follow your purpose because you're afraid of conflict, aggression or defensiveness from others can be crippling. We might avoid conflict at all costs and doubt our ability to handle any conflict that comes our way.
   Statement: *I won't say what I think because I'm afraid people will disagree with me.*

3. **Fear of failure:** Being afraid of not achieving a desired outcome or meeting an expectation you've set for yourself sometimes means we don't even try. This fear of failure

holds us back from pursuing our purpose; instead, we miss opportunities and develop feelings of regret.

Statement: *I won't ask that person on a date because I'll be embarrassed if it doesn't work out.*

4. **Fear of success:** This one may be new to you, but being afraid of success is also a barrier to connecting with your core. When we fear success, we grow anxious and reluctant to work towards our purpose. Instead, we suffer from self-doubt, procrastination and self-sabotage.

    Statement: *I'm not going to put my all into the annual presentation because I might get a promotion, and I don't have the ability to take on such a big job.*

Fear of judgement was something I struggled terribly with. Even though I knew my purpose was to help people find their voice and tell their stories, I was constantly worried about what people would think if I pursued a career that allowed me to do that. I was afraid to step outside the line others had drawn for me and express myself in a way they weren't ready to receive. I found myself quieting my expression and dimming my light to fit into a category that would keep the invisible peace.

It wasn't until my mentor called me out on this fear and into something more substantial – my heart – that I was able to move ahead. She simply said, 'Get over yourself, Janika! It's not about you. It's about the people you're going to help'. Now, some might think this is an odd thing for a mentor to say to her mentee, but she couldn't have put it a better way. I understood what she meant instantly, and she knew it. 'If you can't show up for you,' she added, 'then you have to show up for them.'

Acknowledging the ways your purpose can be used to benefit others should help give you the courage to step out of your fear and into your heart. Armed with this wisdom, I hope you can kickstart your confidence by asking yourself how your purpose can positively impact other people. This will strengthen your core even more because it leverages your heart and uses intentions to link your narratives, expression and stories to that focused purpose.

The service archetypes

When shifting a fear mindset into an act of serving mindset, it may be useful to identify and aligning with one of the service archetypes below.

The teacher: My stories serve by sharing and showing. I'm commonly drawn to narratives where I teach as a form of service.

The healer: My stories serve by easing suffering. I'm commonly drawn to narratives where I heal as a form of service.

The creator: My stories serve by inspiring and nurturing. I'm commonly drawn to narratives where I create as a form of service.

The builder: My stories serve by creating and completing. I'm commonly drawn to narratives where I build as a form of service.

The messenger: My stories serve by sharing and documenting aspects of this human life. I'm commonly drawn to narratives where I share as a form of service.

The guide: My stories serve by leading and showing. I'm commonly drawn to narratives where I provide direction as a form of service.

Linking intentions to your purpose

Until my late twenties, I had no idea how integral intentions were in the journey to become a storyteller. By then, I'd come through a whirlwind of development in the self-development and spiritual sense, and I was beginning to learn how setting intentions could change my life. When I took action that was in alignment with my intentions, they functioned as guides along my story. These experiences were shaping me as a person, and if I'm the lucky one who gets to introduce you to the importance of intention to storytelling, it's an honour!

Intentions are conscious choices to engage in or pursue actions that lead to a desired outcome. They are thoughts that can be captured in any way that best suits you, such as on your phone, a sticky note in your journal or simply repeated in your head. The main thing is that they represent a commitment to a clear plan of action and a way forward to elicit a specific goal.

As I started to become more familiar with the practice of intention setting, I began to dance with what the term meant for me. Naturally, I Googled 'intentions', and it was easy enough to find information on the *benefits* of intention setting, as it's widely discussed. Leaders in various spaces, from self-development to sports and even politics talk about how setting intentions helps them focus their energy and attention on a specific goal. It was how to set intentions that turned out to be harder to research. What constitutes a good intention? What is a bad intention? Was there even such a thing? I explored these questions as I carved out my own definition of a strong intention.

I discovered that in order for an intention to be 'right' for me, I had to be able to integrate it seamlessly into my life and channel it through my expression. In order for that to happen, the intention had to link to my priority purpose. To help me visualise this connection, I pictured a chain or a tube connecting my intention to my purpose and binding the two together. Without this direct chain anchoring my intentions back to my core, they were more like hopes, desires or wishes upon a star. They lacked the oomph to motivate me or keep me committed and focused over time. Only when they connected to my purpose was I ready to take action on them and move forward.

Setting an intention is a necessary step if you want to act in alignment with your purpose. When you bring both of these elements to the fore while expressing yourself, no matter the outcome, you're feel confident in your 'why' and be able to connect to that driving force to enhance your storytelling. Armed with this knowledge, let's look at how to set a solid intention and then link it to your purpose to give it power. Creating a solid intention includes five key steps.

1. **Choose an intention matches your purpose:** Say your priority purpose is 'helping people obtain their physical health goals

so they can live their healthiest life'. Your intention should be something that lines up with physical health and healthy living in some capacity. For example, 'finding a job in the fitness industry.'

2. **Next, make it specific:** Narrow your intention down to the bones of what you're trying to achieve. What specific story outcome do you want as a result of setting this intention? This is where you might sharpen your intention to 'getting a job as a women's trainer at the new local gym'.

3. **Phrase it positively:** The more positive and engaging your intention, the more you'll revisit it. For example, 'getting a job as a personal trainer to help women improve their lives through fitness' is much better than 'I'll try and apply for fitness jobs so I can hopefully help women.'

4. **Visualise it:** When setting an intention, spend time picturing yourself achieving it. Close your eyes and imagine yourself in the situation. Allow yourself to feel as if you're living it. This will connect you to the thoughts, feelings and emotions surrounding your purpose and remind you why you settled on this intention in the first place.

5. **Take action:** Now, go forth! Apply for that job! Take action towards your intention, knowing that every step you make and every narrative you engage with – from your résumé to the

interview, to your very first client – is linked to your greater purpose.

Storyteller session 13:
Set an intention

With your purpose in mind, write down your intention using the prompts below. Feel free to change the words and make it your own. These are just suggestions to get you started. You may find you have to draft a few versions before you land on an intention you're happy with, but that is perfectly okay.

My intention is _____
*to/so*_____ *and/with*_____ .

Congratulations on creating your intention! Now, write it down again and place it somewhere you'll be able to see it a few times throughout the day. Perhaps write it on your favourite colour sticky note and place it on your desk at work. Or, if you'd prefer to connect with it first thing in the morning, stick it to the bathroom mirror. Do whatever works best for you because it's your own!

Now that you've created an intention linked to your purpose, you can then start to act in a purposeful way throughout your day. Once you know your guiding principles, it becomes astonishingly apparent when people you interact with are disconnected from their core or haven't given much thought to their why. You might notice that their stories lack conviction and heart, or fall flat when compared with those of a storyteller who has integrated their core into the way they express themselves. The important stories you share should be told through the lens of this core purpose to keep you connected and grounded in who you are.

Applying step 3 in real life

In this chapter, we've explored the importance of crafting purpose, intention and direction regardless of the fears that hold us back. Now it's time to review how anchoring into your core can be used to benefit your effectiveness as a storyteller in your everyday life.

WORK

It's said that if you love what you do, you'll never work a day in your life. I'm not 100 per cent sold on this quote to be honest. Not many people I know love every aspect of their job all the time, especially on challenging days. Many of my dear friends are nurses and teachers, and what keeps them going through the difficult times is that they are connected to their purpose.

I prefer to say that if you find what you do purposeful and stay connected to your intentions, you won't *mind* working. The same goes if you're an employee, business owner or entrepreneur. If you can connect what you do to your purpose in some capacity, you're laughing. Not only are you laughing, but when you talk about your work or share details about it with others, you'll light up and people will notice. Here's how crafting that strong core strengthens your narratives in business.

Strengthen motivation

Blake Mycoskie, founder of TOMS shoes is an example that demonstrates how being connected to a purpose can drive entrepreneurial success. The company is known for its famous 'one for one' business model where for every pair of shoes purchased, TOMS donates a pair to a child in need. The purpose guiding this business is pretty clear (and remarkable) because Blake wanted to create a sustainable business that could make a meaningful impact on the lives of children.

During a trip to Argentina in 2006, he witnessed children without shoes and became aware of how important footwear was for a person's health. By aligning his business with his purpose, he was able to fuel his motivation and dedicate himself to his cause. Despite the many ongoing challenges of starting a business, establishing a supply chain and spreading brand awareness, this model of 'one for one' kept Blake focused while also captivating the consumer by connecting them to a social cause. TOMS created a movement that resonated with people worldwide who saw his social entrepreneurship and purpose-driven business and wanted to contribute to this greater cause. Blake's personal and professional fulfilment exemplifies the incredible power of purpose-led business.

Real-life application: Keep your employees and/or co-workers motivated when outlining business and/or workplace goals for the next financial year.

Here are five tips on how to keep others motivated when reviewing business goals by connecting and reminding them of the sense of purpose at the heart of the business.

1. **Pick your approach**

    Depending on your business or workplace, you'll want to ensure you pick a time and method to deliver this message in a way that connects to employees/co-workers. An internal email may work for some workplaces, but a sit-down conversation may work better for others. Evaluate the best way to outline the upcoming financial year goals and make a time for it that everyone can attend.

2. **Reflect on success**

    Kick things off by reflecting on the successes of the current year, offering clear examples of how their hard work and dedication has contributed to the business achieving the original purpose or intention of the workplace. This will help the team see how their individual efforts impact the business, environment or industry, etc.

3. **Acknowledge challenges**

    Be honest about what it took to get those successes. Perhaps some of your staff or coworkers had to endure long nights, extra workdays or unpaid labor. Be sure to acknowledge how their actions and sacrifices helped add to the success or result.

4. **Introduce the new goals**

    Highlight the goals for the upcoming financial year and discuss how these goals will contribute towards and benefit the main purpose/intention of the business or workplace.

5. **Confirm the why**

    This is your chance to bring it home and reignite motivation and inspiration among the team to keep people focused and motivated. Highlight the greater purpose their work serves and create a sense of camaraderie and collaboration to support each other on the journey together.

RELATIONSHIPS

Being connected to your core why through your intentions can provide bucket loads of insight into your behaviour. When we open up and share what motivates, drives and inspires us, we shed light on our actions in a way that can deepen our relationships. Suddenly, we make a lot more sense to the person digesting our stories because they understand the greater lens through which we are looking at life. Not only can they see it, but there is also a chance they will be motivated by the very same things, which deepens their connection to us and our self-expression.

Creating unity

Throughout Barack and Michelle Obama's 25 years of marriage and public life, they have always emphasised the importance of partnership and been vocal in their support of the pursuit of each other's individual goals and purposes. While Barack was focused on serving as a political leader, Michelle worked to empower communities through education and the addressing of social issues.

Though Michelle took a temporary backseat when Barack became the first African–American president, she found focus on initiatives like 'Let's Move', which aimed to combat childhood obesity. She continued to communicate her purpose (to her husband and to the world) while serving as the First Lady and supporting Barack in the pursuit of his purpose. The Obama's example highlights that by openly discussing their purposes, they were able to find common ground and support each other's individual journeys while also creating and maintaining a united front as a couple.

Real-life application: Tell your partner you want to change your career

Here are five tips on how to communicate with your partner that you want to change your career to align with your purpose.

1. **Stress-free zone**

    You'll want to make sure you bring this topic up in a time that is suitable for both of you, and preferably during a time that is not particularly stressful or busy for your partner. Your career change may involve you going back to school or limiting the amount of income you can bring into the household, so you'll want to ensure there are no obvious concerns for finances.

2. **Express your purpose**

    Now is your moment to put it all out there for your partner. Clearly communicate your passion for this new career path and explain how it aligns with your greater purpose. Share your reasons for wanting to make this change and how it will positively affect not just you individually, but also your relationship.

3. **Articulate your plan**

    Come ready with a solid plan. Will you go back to school immediately? If so, how will you pay for itthis Or perhaps you have already created the résumé for the new job? Show it to them and articulate how you see this shift playing out.

4. **Seek support and collaboration**

    Explain that you're open to collaborating on what the plan going forward could look like, and hear them out when they share their thoughts. Perhaps there is a potential for compromises that make you both happy.

5. **Be open to discussion**

    Your partner is obviously going to have an opinion and may also have concerns or questions about your career change. Anticipate their doubts and try to answer them as best you can.

SELF

Our thoughts are with us the moment we open our eyes in the morning. They are the stories we engage with and tell ourselves, and they can shift the mood of our entire day before we step out of bed. When we have a solid story core, we can lean on it on long, uncertain or challenging days. By committing our thoughts to a greater sense of direction, we can derive meaning and enjoy greater fulfilment, which in turn improves our mental health and wellbeing.

Remaining inspired

Consider someone who is deeply committed to fighting climate change. Their core is being an environmental activist, and this purpose calls them to protect the planet for generations to come. When faced with setbacks such as political resistance, scrutiny, or slow progress, they derive inspiration and resilience by reflecting upon their intended purpose.

On long days that demand significant time and effort and only garner criticism, they depend on the sense of direction and this long-term perspective of being committed to bettering the planet and protecting it from harm. This sense of purpose allows them to remain true to themselves and find the inspiration to carry on, despite the challenges posed by this huge and complex problem.

Real-life application: Creating an inspiring vision board that illustrates your purpose

Here are five tips to keep in mind when creating a vision board that reflects your purpose.

1. **Be specific and detailed**

    The more specific you can be, the better because the more clear you can get about your vision, the more focused your actions will become. How do you see yourself carrying out your purpose? Who is with you? Where are you? Start turning these visions into a visual collection.

2. **Engage your emotions**

    Choose images and words that evoke a strong emotions within you in order to keep you feeling inspired and engaged. Visualise yourself carrying out your purpose and then reflect on what you're feeling in that moment. Get it all down on your vision board.

3. **Include words of affirmation**

    Incorporate a few sentences or words of affirmation that you can repeat to yourself when gazing at this vision board. These positive statements will serve as powerful reminders of your intentions and keep you inspired and motivated.

4. **Include successes and wins**

    Anytime you experience a success or win related to your purpose, put an image, word or reminder of it on the board. You can always continue adding to your vision board, it's never done!

5. **Have it on display**

    Last, you'll want to place this board somewhere where you can see it often. I keep mine by my desk so I'm reminded of my visions for the future every time I sit down to write or meet with clients. You might enjoy having yours in the space you get ready, or perhaps in your office.

CHAPTER SIX

Step 4: Expressing yourself effectively

> 'If you talk to a man in a language he understands, that goes to his head. If you talk to him in his language, that goes to his heart.'
>
> **Nelson Mandela,** *Activist and Politician*

The importance of communicating effectively is hammered into us from an early age. As toddlers, our parents teach us our first words to help us get our thoughts across. At school, we're taught to speak up in class. And as adults, we might attempt to master the art of public speaking to further our career or give a speech at a friend's wedding. Success can hinge on how well you communicate in the moment, and rightfully so. No matter how interesting your story is, if your communication skills aren't up to snuff, you won't be able to effectively convey your message and intention. And if you can't do that, you'll be forever crawling uphill in a battle to inform, inspire or influence other people.

This is why step four is dedicated to the art of expressing yourself effectively. I bet you've probably interacted with a few people this week who made you think, *Gee, you've got no idea how to communicate.* Maybe you even thought that about yourself after something nonsensical came out of your mouth. Contrast those moments with a time you were listening to someone share their thoughts with clarity, coherence and confidence. I bet they got your attention – in a good way.

Effective communication is so crucial to good storytelling and therefore good relationships, success in business – basically anything involving other people. It's so important that you can do an entire degree in it, like I did. The broad branches of communication touch almost every aspect of human life, from psychology, business and education, to media, politics, art and more. Expressing ourselves effectively is a skill we must keep working at throughout our lives in order to enhance our abilities, build stronger relationships and, ultimately, step into our storytelling power.

Don't just take my word for this. Numerous studies have evaluated the importance of effective communication in human interactions. In 2012, Google set out to answer the question 'what makes a team successful?'. Over the course of a year, they studied hundreds of internal teams within Google in a quest to discover why some thrived at work and others failed.

The findings of that research indicated that effective communication was one of the factors that contributed to a group's success rate. More specifically, team members who communicated openly, illustrated active listening and demonstrated sensitivity with empathy were more effective than others.[4] What's interesting about effective expression is that it's not just talking that is measured, but listening, too. Or, in Google's case, *active* listening and paying attention to the audience to gauge their feelings during a conversation or exchange of stories. Turns out this type of listening is just as important to good communication as talking.

Active listening is something I've always been very good at. It's the focused act of understanding and responding to what someone is saying, both through their words and also their body language. In the past, I was often teased for being too emotional and too quiet. I was told that my soft heart made me weak and that I wouldn't be heard just because I didn't have the loudest voice. I so desperately wanted to be a boss bitch babe who didn't give a f*ck about anything or anyone on her way to achieve her dreams, but that just wasn't me.

Since then, I've learned that the person with the loudest voice is often also the person who starts rambling, and doesn't even notice as everyone else switches off as they beg their brain to block out the droning, booming voice. Just because someone speaks loudly doesn't mean there's emotional connection behind their words.

This emotional connection is precisely what sets me apart as a storyteller. I have an ability to connect my message to the hearts of others, though it took me a long time to realise this. A key difference between expression and *effective* expression is in the case of the latter, the heart and head work together. There is no one-size-fits-all when it comes to communication, which is why you need to use your heart to search for common ground or evoke an emotion that will help your message or story have impact.

When you communicate, you should strive to express yourself in your own unique way, and for that unique audience. It's important to lean into what makes you comfortable and learn how to honour that while expressing yourself. In this chapter, we'll explore how various communication styles thread together to help us tell a story. You may feel a particular affinity with one style or perhaps more skilled in one area than another.

After discussing these styles, I'll introduce you to the secret weapon that has elevated my ability to express myself effectively more than anything else. I didn't discover it while doing my university communications degree, but it really works, and I can't wait to show you how to apply it.

What's your communication flava?

You know that saying, *'A picture is worth a thousand words'*? Well, whoever came up with it was really onto something. We often assume the only way to get a message across is to express ourselves verbally, but research shows that we take in huge amounts of information visually, and through our other senses – often more than we hear. For example, in the middle of talking to someone, you might become aware that you are simultaneously communicating with them in different ways. That's because we use four main communication channels: verbal, written, non-verbal and visual. How effectively you convey and receive messages can either help or hinder your storytelling. Let's dive into these communication channels now. See if you can identify the ones that come easily to you and any you struggle with.

Verbal communication

You've been practising this since you were a wee one. This form uses spoken words and sounds to convey a message to an audience, and it's everywhere, from our face-to-face conversations, phone calls, voice memos, presentations, movies, songs, radio, meetings, speeches, announcements, video posts . . . Language and sound communicate our thoughts, ideas and feelings to another person, group of people or maybe even the world (hello, social media! I'm looking at you).

In order for verbal communication to be most effective, not only do you have to express yourself well, but you also need to be able to understand and interpret verbal and non-verbal cues from whomever you happen to be interacting with. Which brings me to the next form of communication . . .

Non-verbal communication

This is the channel of communication that trips people up the most. If you've ever interacted with someone who has terrible non-verbal communication skills, you can probably guess why: their physical cues can often be more confusing than anything coming out of their mouth. In my past life as a marketing executive, I had a client who was a verbal comms ninja. She was an expert at simplifying complex ideas and capable of using language to brilliant effect, but in person, her facial expressions and body language let her communication skills down.

During a meeting to discuss branding concepts with me and one of the designers on my team, this client said that she loved the design direction we were showing her, but her face told a different story. Each time the designer placed a new image in front of her, she scrunched up her face and shook her head with disgust – all while saying how much she liked it! We tried to keep going, but the two of us were so confused that we finally had to stop the presentation to ask the client what her deal was.

Turned out that she was utterly unaware that her physical reactions were telling a different story to her words. She explained that the reason for her entertaining faces was that she was comparing our designs to that of a previous agency – one she'd paid a lot of money to. She was annoyed that she'd spent so much money on work she didn't enjoy nearly as much as this new branding. (Phew! Could have fooled us!)

That's the thing about non-verbal communication: it transmits information intentionally and unintentionally. The amount of information that flows through our gestures, facial expressions, tone of voice, and body language is huge. It can contradict or complement what is being discussed without us saying a word. Never underestimate its importance.

Active listening is also an essential part of understanding non-verbal cues when someone else is speaking. By paying close attention to them, you can digest all the messages coming your way and ensure that you communicate effectively when you respond. Maintaining eye contact while listening allows you to pick up on a person's non-verbal cues and respond naturally. Asking questions at the right time and then summarising the main points of whatever was shared are good ways to practice active listening.

Written communication

Similar to verbal communication, written communication refers to the exchange of information, thoughts and ideas through language – either in the form of written symbols or text. The digital age has meant we've all had to polish our written communication skills to ensure we express ourselves and in a clear and concise manner when we send text messages, emails, letters, cards, reports or post on social media.

Solid written communication skills are so essential that many employers list it as a prerequisite for many jobs. Excelling at this skill goes beyond good grammar and spelling; understanding clarity, tone and context are also incredibly important if you want to ensure the person reading your words understands them, and that the message they receive is the same one you intended to send.

Visual communication

Visual communication relies solely on the exchange of visual elements to convey messages. It employs a wide range of mediums such as images, presentations, art, videos, diagrams, and likewise aids to present and communicate information in an optical format. By communicating visually, elements such as colors, typography, and design principles can enhance comprehension and engage your audience. At times, visual communication can transcend language barriers, serving as a universal language that can be understood and interpreted by people from diverse cultures and backgrounds.

It has the ability to condense information into digestible formats like infographics, charts, and diagrams that facilitate efficient and simplified delivery of messages.

***

Under the two major umbrellas of written and verbal communication exists a vast spectrum of sub-styles, which we'll explore in more depth in the storyteller session coming up. For now, let's focus on the two styles that occupy opposite ends of the communication spectrum: formal and informal. The use of each of these styles is dictated by a few different factors: the person or group doing the communicating, their intended audience and the context the communication is happening within. Each style has its own conventions and rules.

Formal communication

Formal communication is often used by institutions (e.g., churches, universities), certain professions (e.g. medicine or law) or called for in special circumstances (such as a wedding invitations or funerals). It is mostly written, but can also be verbal. The language used is specific to the rules, etiquette and conventions of the person or group doing the communicating: academia, government, or corporate workplaces, for example. The person tasked with crafting a formal message will typically display a high degree of professionalism, because this type of messaging requires in-depth knowledge of the conventions and structure that need to be followed.

Informal communication

This style of communication can also be verbal or written. It's the most casual and relaxed style of expression of all, and best suited to intimate settings with close family, good friends or groups of like-minded people. Depending on the context and people involved, anything goes, including slang, humour, profanity and incorrect spelling and use of grammar. This is the dominant style of communication on social media apps such as TikTok and Instagram.

Storyteller session 14:
Pinpointing your communication style

In addition to these forms of communication, there are many other styles of communicating, and each of us has one or two that we naturally gravitate to. Review the communication styles used in the scenario below and tick the ones that echo the styles you use most frequently.

Scenario:
A coworker consistently interrupts you during meetings at work.

Communication styles

Direct: Straightforward, concise and to the point. Doesn't beat around the bush.

'I would like to address the issue of Jenny's continual interruption during our team meetings. It happens often and it's disrupting the flow of our discussions. Let's allow each person to finish speaking before jumping in to make sure we're all heard.'

Indirect: Uses subtle hints and clues to point towards a message.

'Sometimes during our meetings it's hard to keep the conversation flowing because of interruptions. It might be best if we have a more structured approach to meetings to ensure everyone gets a chance to speak and be heard.'

Aggressive: A forceful, intimidating and commanding way of getting a message across. At times, without regard for another's feelings or opinions.

'I am sick and tired of being interrupted by you, Jenny. You always do this in team meetings! It's inconsiderate and you obviously have no regard for me or my opinions. Learn some basic manners.'

Assertive: A confident, concise style of expressing thoughts and feelings without bending to another's point of view.

'Jenny, I've noticed that you often interrupt me during our team meetings, and I want to address this now. I would appreciate it if next time you wait until I'm finished making my point and sharing my opinion before you jump in with yours.'

Passive aggressive: Avoiding direct confrontation and instead subtly expressing your hostility or annoyance via sarcasm, gossiping or sabotaging.

> On the way out of the meeting a colleague says, 'Florence made some good points, didn't she?' You nod, but mutter under your breath, 'I wouldn't know, I couldn't hear her with Jenny hogging the spotlight for most of the time.'

Passive: Avoiding conflict and remaining timid without standing up for yourself or expressing your needs.

> 'Thanks, Jenny for those points you made in the meeting. You always say it much better than I can.' *Starts looking for a new job rather than address the issue.*

Can you identify which channel and style of communication you use most frequently? Taking time to do this is important because our communication preferences reflect our approach to expressing ourselves and how we showcase our unique personalities and priorities in co interpersonal interactions. It's worth getting curious about why you tend to lean on a particular style. Does the style you currently use align with the way you want to express yourself. If not, which communication styles you would *like* to use in the future? Are there any you admire when you observe others communicating? If you want to shift to a style that doesn't come naturally to you, remember that refining it is all about practice. Actively make the choice to show up in that communication style and you'll improve a little each time you attempt it.

Bonus communication channel: Tuning into the vibe

I swear I could write a whole other book on this channel of communication, so buckle up because I'm about to do my best to summarise it for you. This is the secret weapon I spoke of earlier; the one I credited for making me a more effective communicator, and now I'm going to share it with you. It's called vibrational energy and it's very likely that you're already using to your advantage (or disadvantage). Now, before you start rolling your eyes at the term 'vibrational' thinking it's some 'woo-woo' notion, please hear me out because there's good solid science behind it.

Every single thing in this universe is made up of molecules and atoms that are in constant motion. The movement from these creates a vibrational energy that can be measured in frequency. This means every thought we have, emotion we feel and action we take contributes to creating a vibrational energy around us.

We *feel energy*, too. It gets transferred between molecules whenever they collide or are absorbed. When you're telling a story to someone, you can bet there is an exchange of energy happening. This is how we are able to feel an energetic frequency with someone without having to say a word.

Vibrational energy is the reason you can instantly dislike a stranger or feel an immense pull towards them, without knowing why. You're picking up on their vibration and the space they occupy (otherwise known as their energetic field), and depending on the vibe in their field, their story may land or bomb with you for no other reason than 'the vibe wasn't good'. Our energetic fields speak volumes about us, and if our vibrational frequency is consistently low, it's likely that the negative thoughts and feelings we're sitting in are negatively affecting our frequency.

I bet you've noticed how – in your own life – you feel so much better when you spend time with someone who is positive, joyful and passionate versus a person who is angry, resentful or frustrated. Of course, acknowledging and honouring our true feelings, even the bad ones, is essential, but if we stay in a state of low vibrational thinking for too long, we risk dragging down our storytelling power in unintentional ways.

The Law of Attraction we spoke of earlier further supports this idea. This law becomes obvious on those days when you feel like nothing is going right. Ever try to express yourself on a day when you're feeling particularly low vibe? It's a disaster! Let's use Lilly and Hailey to showcase the law of attraction in storytelling action.

Low-vibe Lily

Lily opens her eyes, which feel heavy as cement because she didn't get enough sleep last night. She curses her habit of binging *Netflix* until midnight, especially when she knew today was so important. She should have used the hours she spent watching true crime documentaries to prepare for the speech she's expected to give at work. A feeling of shame pings in her core and she scolds herself, *Why do I always do this?*

To distract herself from this unpleasant emotion, she grabs her phone and scrolls for 20 minutes before getting up. The algorithm knows she's interested in ultra-clean, tidy homes and puts on a ripper of a show. She notices her room is a pigsty and starts feeling guilty that her home isn't as perfect as the ones she's just been looking at on her device. In the bathroom, her inner voice starts to roar as she looks in the mirror and locks eyes with the person standing before her. *What the hell were you thinking putting your hand up for this presentation? You're a terrible public speaker! Not to mention you look like shit today. You'll embarrass the living daylights out of yourself and forget the specifics. What if Sarah from accounts is there? She'll have a field day watching you screw this up.*

With these thoughts ringing in her head, Lily leaves home feeling a mixture of low-vibrational fear, shame, guilt and anxiety about her speech and her life. She walks into the meeting room and blurts out her presentation as fast as she can, without pausing between PowerPoint slides or making eye contact with her colleagues. (Oh, look! There's Sarah from accounts.)

As Lily predicted, her audience wasn't particularly interested or engaged in her presentation, and that's a pity because she actually did a great job on the slides and clearly knew her stuff. Even so, her colleagues couldn't help but feel that she was 'off' thanks to the low-vibrational energy she brought into the room with her. Lily slinks back to her desk disappointed in herself and embarrassed that she didn't blow everyone away with her work the way she'd hoped to when she volunteered to take this on.

High-vibe Hailey

The sun peaks through the windows and wakes Hailey up before her alarm. She takes a minute to watch the golden ripples of light move around the room, feeling thankful for her night of restful sleep. Today is a big day at work, and she feels good about the presentation that is printed and ready to go on her desk. She may not know everything about the financials, but she's excited at the prospect of running this meeting for the first time.

On the way out of the house, she gives herself a high-five in the mirror. *You've got this!* she tells herself confidently. As she turns towards the door, she stubs her toe on the coffee table and lets out a big ol' swear word. When the pain subsides, she accepts that this happened, and then lets the frustration go with the thought, *Ah, well. Shit happens!*

In the meeting room, she spots Sarah from accounts. She's not the most pleasant person on the team, but Hailey makes an effort to smile at her anyway. Once everyone is seated, she gets behind the podium, takes a deep breath, calls in courage and goes for it. Hailey keeps her self-talk positive while delivering the presentation, and even though she doesn't know the answers to all the questions she fields at the end of her presentation, she's thankful that people paid attention and answers them the best she can. Her team are impressed by her ability to engage a room, and even Sarah stops by to tell her she did a good job.

Both of these ladies used the secret weapon, but only Hailey used it to her advantage to express herself. By reaching for high vibrational thoughts and feelings before, during and after her presentation, Hailey was able to keep her vibration high and convey that in the room. As Hailey pointed out after stubbing her toe, sometimes, shit happens. And, while it's important to acknowledge true feelings when they come up, it's also important not to dwell on them. Hailey only indulged in her negative feelings of pain and anger for a few minutes. Instead of holding onto that frustration all day, she switched gears and reached for the higher feeling of acceptance.

This is the key to the secret weapon, and the lesson that I want you to take from these examples. If you're in a low-vibration mood or experiencing negative thoughts, remember that you have options! Make the effort to reach for a feeling with a higher vibration. Sometimes, this tiny adjustment can make all the difference to the story we tell ourselves, and consequently, the story that others pick up from our non-verbal cues and vibrational energy.

Storyteller session 15:
Reach for a higher vibration

Remember, even if you only make one slight change to your feelings, that's okay! This can make all the difference in your storytelling. Review the list below and come back to it should you need to reach for a higher vibration. If you're feeling one of the lower emotions, look for one that is slightly higher and try to swap it.

High vibrational
Joy, love, excitement, passion, gratitude

Neutral vibrational
Ease, acceptance, hope, willingness, courage

Low vibrational
Frustration, worry, sadness, boredom, jealousy

Very low vibrational
Fear, anxiery, guilt, shame, despair

The art of expressing yourself

Storytelling is an art that we've practised collectively as a species for thousands of years, so there's a well-trodden formula for making stories more compelling, and thankfully for us, it's straightforward: Setting + character + theme + conflict + plot = riveting tale! In this section, we'll look at three crucial story elements – setting, character and what I like to call 'the 'why' – and how they combine to create magic. As you'll see, having a deep understanding of the three previous steps in this book is essential to mastering the art of storytelling, because each of those steps echoes one of the three elements.

> **Setting = Step one** Holding space for your narratives
> **Character = Step two** Knowing who you (truly) are
> **The 'why' = Step three** Crafting a strong purpose

Enhancing each of these story elements is crucial if you want to create a strong narrative that captures your audience's attention. As we discuss each of these three elements in more detail, I'll share some tips you can use to strengthen them, whether you're telling a story about your favourite dog breed or sharing strong political views.

Story element 1: Setting

Have you ever watched a movie and been so confused by the setting that you completely miss the quirky traits of the characters, not to mention their dialogue or stories? Me too! Unclear setting is one of my biggest pet peeves when it comes to movies and books. The same goes for storytelling in everyday life. If we're talking, please give me context for your story so I don't sit there scratching my head. A few simple facts will let your audience know where and when this story takes place, who is involved and why you are telling it in the first place.

Tips for strengthening setting: If you're trying to connect people to a story from your childhood, pull in descriptive elements that paint a picture of that era, such as the technology, music or fashion. Context provides a solid stage for the characters (likely you) and their actions. It also helps your audience to orient themselves mentally in that time and place, and then relax and submit to your storytelling and its desired outcome instead of thinking, *Huh?* the whole way through it.

A compelling setting creates a mood and builds the atmosphere your story will live in. Your audience will take cues from your descriptions and if they are good, they'll be right there in the story with you. Tell them what you hear, see, smell, taste, or touch? Use specific details to create vivid connections and immersive experiences so your audience sees from your point of view.

Story element 2. Character
Good storytellers are able to tell engaging stories, but a great storyteller can make you see yourself in their stories, and this is because their characters are compelling – especially their protagonist. Also known as the main character, the protagonist is often the most crucial element in any narrative. They often have qualities, thoughts and emotions that the audience can relate to, making it easier for them to care about this character and identify with their message.

Tips for strengthening character: To create a strong protagonist in your own story, you've got to unpack their feelings and emotions and express them in an honest and unfiltered way. This allows the audience to understand and empathise with the protagonist's actions and the decisions they make so they invest in the story. Chances are, when you express emotion honestly through the lens of a strong character, your audience will connect to your story on a deeper level.

Story element 3: The 'why'

Another layer in the art of expressing a story is championing the 'why' – aka your story's purpose or core. Aka, it's theme. You've got to (succinctly) tell people why you care about sharing this story, and, more importantly, why *they* should care enough to follow it. We're a fickle bunch these days, and so easily distracted in this content economy. To hold someone's attention, you've really got to wow them, and then keep their attention. A tried-and-true way of showcasing a story's why is by highlighting the challenge and the chase. Challenge (or conflict) is whatever problem, issue, frustration, or experience is being faced in your story. Chase (or plot) is the journey through, around or over that challenge.

Tip for getting your 'why' across: Knowing how to balance the two elements of challenge and chase is where the art of expressing a story comes in. Bog your audience down in the details of the challenge and you risk losing them. Make your story all about the chase without adequately digging into the challenge, and they won't be invested enough to follow along.

We are used to consuming narratives, and this has trained us to want to see a story arc from point A to point B. But we also want to understand why we're on this arc to begin with so we can connect to it on an emotional level. The more relatable and honest the challenge is, the easier it is to make it compelling. Introduce it at the start, and then promptly move into the chase. Even if the ending you give the audience is not entirely buttoned up, at least the story has moved forwards (or backwards) in a way that's kept them invested.

Include each of these elements in your stories, and apply the tips I've shared to enhance how you express them. Be sure to avoid ambiguity, overgeneralising, inconsistency and a lack of clarity, and if a story doesn't engage or land the way you intended, cross-reference it against these elements. Was anything missing? Was the balance between the challenge and chase off? See where you might refine the narrative so you can express it more effectively next time.

Assessing your audience

Before we head into the book's last step, let's pause to discuss the importance of assessing your audience. Remember how I said active listening was an important piece of effective communication? Well, it really is, and that's because you need to *know* what your audience wants to hear and how to express yourself in the way they'll be most receptive to. Understanding who you are speaking to and what matters to them is going to help you craft the most compelling narrative – one where you can tailor your message to their specific interests, needs, preferences and motivations. This was one of the biggest lessons I learned in my career, so I want to highlight it again so you can either write it down, bookmark this page or rip it out and keep with you. (I'm dead serious.)

Understanding your audience and tailoring your storytelling to them WILL make you a better storyteller AND move you closer to your desired outcome.

As valuable as this learning has been to me, it isn't without its controversies. In my mid-twenties I was at an interview for a job that sounded too good to be true. I was desperate to get out of a role that wasn't paying enough money, and was shocked when the interviewer told me that the salary for the successful candidate would be double what I was currently being paid. Not only was the money better, but the benefits were also desirable. As much as I hated going to the dentist, I'd almost have to go with benefits this good!

I wanted this job so badly that (big surprise) I used my storytelling power to create a killer resume, secure an interview and get the job. Once I became the company's marketing strategist, I had multiple touchpoints with employees in all different departments, including the big boss (let's call him Mike). Though I didn't converse with Mike often, I occasionally braved his daunting hyper-masculine office – usually to ask for extra funding for my department or approval on a campaign. Other times, I was there for my quarterly performance review.

During one of these quarterly performance reviews, we recapped on the successful quarter my team had had. Mike ran through my achievements as well as numerous positive comments from senior staff members who worked alongside me, then he smirked and said he had just one additional piece of feedback to give me.

I remember this vividly because I was certain the review would be a positive one, but the look he gave me stopped me in my tracks. It was the sort of look someone might give you before they hit you over the head. Mike proceeded to tell me that, although my work was good, sometimes he wondered if I was being sincere. 'You seem to say all the right things to me, and everyone else in our meetings for that matter.' Then he laughed while recalling times people had been 'eating out of my hand' after I pitched an idea or made a formal request for something.

'The thing is,' Mike continued, 'the reason people respect me is because I'm more honest than that. I can be very abrasive, but perhaps you should try being more honest, too.' I was completely taken aback, and I had to make a conscious effort to stop my bottom lip from twitching. The truth was, hardly anyone at the company liked Mike's 'honesty'. He was a bulldozer, and part of that 'old boys club', so naturally, when he spat orders at people, he believed they were connecting to his 'truth', but what they were really responding to was his position of power. Behind his back, employees bitched about his arrogance all the time.

Mike was watching me carefully, and I could tell he wanted a reaction from me. I sensed that he wanted to shoot down my confidence and make me question my ability to ask for what I wanted. Perhaps he thought I'd cower in my chair or slink away and then send him a weak email about the matter later. That wasn't happening. Instead, I spoke up.

'Mike, as the head marketing strategist my job is to tell stories that connect to a target market. I've been doing this for a long time, so if it appears that I always get my way or always land a pitch, that's because I'm good at tailoring my messaging to suit the audience.' I could see I had his attention.

'It's not that I'm being dishonest or insincere,' I continued, 'I'm delivering the same message as other people, but in a way that makes my audience listen and then motivates them or allows them to see themselves in my story.'

Mike nodded, and said he was impressed with my answer. Perhaps I seemed more sincere to him at that moment, but really, I was just doing what I always did: telling a story from a place of truth and tailoring it to my audience. He just couldn't see or understand that because he used the same loudspeaker to communicate with everyone, which was why people were less receptive to him. They did what he said, but only because he was the boss.

I share this story because it's a great example of assessing your audience and understanding their motivations and desires can help you find the most effective way of reaching them. By understanding what motivates, inspires and interests someone, you can filter your message through that lens. I didn't know Mike personally, but I did know that he respected it when people stood up for themselves, used manners and sounded sure of their opinion. I knew that if I could show up verbally, directly yet politely in that moment, he'd respond positively.

I want to stress that this isn't about you changing your priority purpose or the intention that supports it. This is about you connecting the right audience with the right message. It's also about determining which method of expression best suits that audience. How I connect with another entrepreneur on Instagram is not the same way I'd connect with Jane from accounts. Tailor your chosen form of expression to suit the individual scenario.

Applying step 4 in real life

In this chapter, we explored the role of expression and how important it is to communicate in a way that connects the audience to your message. How you tell a story affects how it's received, and what the outcome will be – it will either draw others in or push them away. Let's look at some examples of how expressing yourself effectively can benefit the narrative of your life.

WORK

Effective expression is non-negotiable in the business world. In professional setting, you have to be able to communicate ideas clearly in order to elicit a specific outcome. It's glaringly obvious when one person in the workplace is a terrible communicator because the whole team often suffers when they have to compensate for that colleague's lack of skill. I bet you can think of a co-worker or boss with terrible communication skills right this very second. On the other hand, being a great communicator can really open doors of opportunity. Let's continue diving into how effectively expressing your stories can assist you in the gaining new business.

Effective networking

At a conference for professionals in her industry, Claire runs into her friend Hannah. During lunch they are told that those who want to continue the discussion from the last lecture can head over to the breakaway room. When Claire asks Hannah if she wants to join, she replies that she'd rather die (she's dramatic like that).

Even though she doesn't know anyone going into the room, Claire decides to join them because she knows how important these events can be. Not only can she spread awareness about the virtual assistant services she offers, potentially gaining more clients, but she might also be able to form connections with others in the industry. Walking into the room, Claire spots a large group engaged in conversation. Rather than stick to the outside of the room, she decides to introduce herself and join their conversation. Turns out, they all work at different companies, and when they ask Claire what she does, they are eager to hear about her business.

Because Claire took time to prepare for this conference, she is able to rattle off a clear and concise pitch that confidently highlights her role, skills and experience. It's well received, and sparks more conversation. Claire actively listens and articulates her questions and comments in a way that seems genuine, relevant and suitable to the environment (direct, friendly, yet professional). She knows how to read the room and so when she starts to feel like her audience is loosing focus and becoming distracted, she stops her pitch so she doesn't oversell herself and bore the group.

Claire is pleasantly surprised when several members of the group ask for her business card after the breakout session concludes. One of the women even says she plans to share Claire's details with a friend who is currently looking for a virtual assistant. In this scenario, Claire's effective way expressing herself results in her gaining new contacts and drumming up potential business. Had she not braved the breakout room on her own or prepared a pitch ahead of time, these opportunities would have been missed. This is a great example of what polished networking skills look like. Claire takes initiative to talk to strangers, knows how to express herself effectively, has you're a clear communication style and is able to read the room.

Real-life application: Nail a networking event
Here are five tips on how to successfully network at an event.

1. **Research the guest list**
   In the weeks or days before the event, actively seek out information on the types of people who will be there. Find out if there are any key players you should introduce yourself to on the day. Use social media, tagged photos and the events website to gain insight into this.

2. **Prepare a pitch**
   As Claire did in the previous example, it's a good idea to have a clear elevator pitch that highlights who you are, your skills, experience and what you bring to the table. Having this planned out and well-rehearsed will help you call it to mind if you find yourself nervous in the situation. Ensure you tailor the pitch to your audience each time by keeping in mind who you're talking to and what their specific needs and interests are.

3. **Take a breath**
   Networking events can feel unnatural because talking to strangers can be daunting. Take a deep breath before you walk up to a group of people and remind yourself that

they probably feel the same as you and will likely just be grateful you came up to them.

4. **Be genuine and professional**
   Networking is about building relationships and sharing stories, so it's important to be authentic and genuine. You'll want to remain professional and show an interest in others by actively listening to them.

5. **Follow up**
   Exchange contact details with people you meet and follow up after the event with a friendly email, text or LinkedIn message. Networking is an ongoing process and building strong relationships requires effort.

RELATIONSHIPS

To create, maintain and enjoy healthy relationships, you must consistently practice effective modes of expressing yourself. We want to be close to our friends, partners, parents and neighbours, and the best way to do this is to communicate and express our inner feelings to the best of our ability. By sharing our thoughts, feelings, needs, and desires clearly and concisely, we're able to establish healthy communication patterns and get our desired message across most of the time.

Promoting healthy discussion

In the TV show *Friends*, the characters of Monica and Chandler experience fertility problems, and discuss adoption as a route to parenthood. Monica expresses her strong desire to be a mother and brings up adoption as a potential avenue for them. She is very excited about adopting a baby, but Chandler is hesitant and feels unsure about the idea. Instead of ignoring their conflicting emotions or arguing, they engage in an honest and healthy discussion around the topic, and dive into their fears, concerns and hopes around adoption.

By expressing themselves and actively listening to each other's perspectives, they allow room for both of their feelings to be heard and respected. It's through this type of healthy, open discussion that they eventually find common ground develop a plan that works for both of them.

Real-life application: Have a discussion with friend/partner on a topic that you disagree on

Here are five tips on how to have a discussion on a topic that you disagree on with someone close to you.

1. **Be respectful**

    Before offering your opinions, reasons you disagree and opposing views, actively listen to the other person's perspective. By showing a genuine interest in what they have to say and asking questions to clarify anything you don't understand, you can ensure that you've digested their point of view. Engaging with their opinions and feelings demonstrates that you value their opinion and creates an inviting atmosphere for the conversation to continue.

2. **Stay calm and composed**

    When it's your turn to share, express yourself effectively. To do this, you'll want to stay calm and composed so you can think clearly and get your perspective across. Take deep breaths when necessary, and try to maintain a neutral tone, even if the conversation becomes heated.

3. **Use 'I' statements**

    When expressing your thoughts and perspective, use 'I' statements like 'I feel like' to express these viewpoints without attacking the other person.

4. **Hear them out**

    Allow them the opportunity to voice their perspective again after you've expressed yourself. This will continue the flow of openness and help promote a healthy discussion.

5. **Find common ground**

    Throughout the conversation see if you can identify things you agree on or shared values to build upon. Emphasise these points of agreement before addressing the areas of disagreement.

SELF

Expressing yourself well is a major tool when it comes to personal growth and self-development, particularly when done authentically and honestly because this sets your truth free. Learning to express yourself effectively builds confidence that no matter the message, you'll be able to deliver it in a way that benefits your situation.

Improving mental health

Having strong mental health is one of the best ways to ensure you are able to express yourself effectively. And mental health can be strengthened through the act of journaling. By taking time to reflect, and then documenting your feelings, we are better able to release negative emotions releasing and cultivate gratitude. Putting feelings and thoughts on paper helps us feel like we've got things out of our system, and we're better off when we do that. Numerous studies show that expressing your feelings in writing can reduce stress levels and improve overall emotional well-being.

Imagine you're feeling stressed out because you're under the pump with your current workload. You've been trying to just put your head down and get through it, but you're starting to notice that the feelings of overwhelm are escalating. By not taking time to express how overwhelmed you are, you are trying to ignore your feelings. You decide it's finally time to get your feelings out in your journal. You're a private person, after all. As you start jotting down the reality of your situation and how it's making you feel, you realise that you were keeping a lot more in than you thought. You've been avoiding yourself, and by taking the time to self-reflect and then express yourself effectively in this journal, you're able to address your emotions and take proactive steps towards managing the stress.

Real-life application: Journaling to get it all out there

Here are five tips on how to express yourself effectively in your journal.

1. **Do it regularly**

   Dedicate a specific amount of time to the practice of journaling that suits you and decide how often you will do this. It can be once a day or once a week, but consistency is key when building a habit. When you do write, use the opportunity to express yourself freely and honestly.

2. **Have a routine**

    It helps to have a particular routine surrounding this new habit. You might use a certain notepad, light your favourite candle, and maybe pop on some meditation music to help you get comfortable and more able to check-in with how you're feeling so you can express it.

3. **Remove judgement**

    Write freely and without judgment. Your journal is a safe space where you can express your true thoughts, feelings and ideas as you see fit. No one else has to read it unless you choose to share.

4. **Use prompts or exercises**

    To get started, you may want to try using writing prompts to open you up to self-expression and deepen self-reflection. You can find these types of prompts online or in books about writing, or you can create your own.

5. **Try different styles**

    Journaling isn't one-size-fits-all. You can choose from stream of consciousness' journaling, bullet journaling, gratitude journaling, reflective journaling . . . The list goes on. Try a few different styles to find one that works with how you like to express yourself.

CHAPTER SEVEN

Step 5: Conquering the storytelling pitfalls

'Can you look without the voice in your head commenting, drawing conclusions, comparing, or trying to figure something out?'[5]
Eckhart Tolle, *Author and Teacher*

If you're anything like me, you envision the final step of any process as the ruby red cherry on top – the extra treat you get to enjoy after completing the hard work. You may also assume that the last step will be the easiest of the bunch (I know I always do). It wasn't until I started writing this chapter that I realised this step is actually the most challenging of the lot, so you'll definitely need the solid foundational structure the previous four steps have given you to help you from falling victim to the common pitfalls we'll explore in this chapter.

It's perfectly normal to experience bouts of courage and determination in life. These are the moments that help us decide when it's time to hand in our notice, have that conversation with our boss or finally speak up and tell our partner what we need. They are prompted by our emotions and give us the surges of bravery we need to get honest with ourselves about what the truth of the matter is.

Each of us is capable of identifying and pursuing the narratives we desire by implementing the lessons we've explored in the first four steps of this book. And, as you're probably now aware, you can use storytelling to propel you in the direction of those desired narratives. The hardest step is showing up every day *in* that story, and *for* that story. Finding the strength to stand firm in your truth and stay consistent with the telling of whatever narrative you've chosen can be downright exhausting. Especially at first.

At the start of this book, I promised these five steps would enable you to harness your narratives and take charge of your life, but I never said they would be easy one hundred percent of the time. After all, it's hard to be a storyteller in a world that prefers uniformity. There are traps designed to keep us quiet and in our place (both psychologically and physically), and these are the pitfalls you'll need to avoid if you want to continue strengthening your power. Closing your eyes and skipping through life hoping you won't fall into one of these traps isn't a good tactic. A much more proactive approach is learning how spot these pitfalls so you can calmly side-step them and also conquer them should you fall in.

You might get to a place in life where you're able to actively share your story in a powerful way, but at that point, it's likely you'll have to serve it on a platter for all of humanity to consume, and the conditions of that exchange are not always pretty. Occasionally, you might fall deep into a pit and have to expend precious emotional energy clawing your way out. For some, crawling out proves too hard, so instead they turn that pit into a comfortable new home that they adjust to, like a hermit crab choosing a new shell.

I know what that's like because I experienced exactly this when I first started storytelling on certain social media platforms, I can't tell you how many times I fell into the pitfalls of the ego and imposter syndrome. Even though I was comfortable expressing myself, digital immortality scared the bejesus out of me. *What if I make a fool out of myself online and that mistake follows me forever?* This thought terrified me, and so did my inability to control where my message went and who heard it. Putting my stories out into the world for people to consume meant I'd be exposed to people who didn't connect to my message or understand my purpose. Still, I knew I needed to be in these online social spaces if I hoped to achieve my goal of reaching more people with my message and purpose. But that didn't make falling into these traps any less painful.

After posting online, I'd spend hours fixating on small stuff like who liked the post or what comments were left, unaware that I hadn't just tumbled into a pit, I was now residing inside it – putting up curtains and making a cup of tea. Being caught up in these mind games was causing my message to be snuffed out because I couldn't keep the flames of it lit long enough to create a fire in the people who needed to feel it. I'd start strong, and share a message using the principles of the four steps, only to be knocked back when a reaction or comment I perceived as negative made me question myself and prompted me to begin telling myself stories that didn't serve me. It was safer inside this cave, but my voice was muffled, and my message silenced. Once I realised this, I knew it was time to crawl out and brave the world again. And now, I'm going to show you why you should do the same.

So, welcome to the storytelling pitfalls. You'll know them by the pits in your stomach. They can start relatively small but be warned, they can expand and suck you (and your story) in. Swallowing your expression whole. By introducing you to some common pitfalls, I hope you'll be able to identify them in the future and, hopefully, avoid them. This is the last step before you embrace your storytelling power. Let's go!

Pitfall 1: The self-sabotaging ego

Depending on who you ask, you'll get different answers to the question, 'What is ego?'. Your friend might explain it as the egotistical wanker she went on a date with. The guy who spoke over her the whole night and wouldn't let her order her own meal. If you've got a psychologist in your trusted circle, they might explain ego as the identity of self and sense of self-worth that individuals develop through their interactions with the external world and their internal thoughts and emotions. If you lean in a more spiritual direction, you may have read Eckhart Tolle's book *The Power of Now*, in which he talks about the ego being something we need to detach from in order to identify with our essence. Since we've been talking about storytelling this entire time, allow me to share my definition of ego – it's a little different, but I think it might help you better understand how it relates to personal narratives.

Ego often gets a bad rap, but it's really just a defence mechanism designed to keep you as safe and comfortable as possible. Think of your ego as a storyteller; it's the voice feeding you particular narratives in an effort to protect you. It's really that simple. When we're fearful, our true self is likely to tap out, so our ego taps in – ready to fight on our behalf while our more vulnerable self crawls to safety. The problem arises when the ego starts to share narratives that are inaccurate or that keep you from experiencing things you need to face in order to grow and progress. Let's look at a few examples of ego at work using the four fears I showed you in Step three.

1. **Fear of judgement**

    The situation: That 'egotistical wanker' who took your girlfriend out to dinner was actually really nervous about meeting your friend. He feared she'd judge him for not being as wealthy or exciting as she is. He was so afraid she'd perceive him as 'not enough' that his ego tapped in and took his true self out of the situation.

    The ego's story: *Wow her with all the amazingly interesting things you've done, and then order the most expensive thing on the menu for her. Don't give her a chance to find out you're a bit of a loser.*

    A better story: If he could have turned down the volume on his ego, he might have been able to calm down enough to hear a different story from his true self: *Just be yourself. Don't try to be anything other than who you are. If she likes you for that, then you'll know it's a match.*

5 STEPS TO STORYTELLING POWER

2. **Fear of conflict**

   The situation: You've lost touch with a friend over the years following a disagreement, and your friendship has taken a hit. You know you should call her to discuss things; after all, you've been friends for years! But you're afraid of what she might say, and worried about damaging the friendship even more.

   The ego's story: *Don't even bother calling Julie. She's so wrapped up in her own world and so selfish that she won't even understand your point of view. It's not worth it.*

   A better story: *Have an honest and transparent conversation with your friend. If the friendship is as important as you think it is, then it's worth risking an uncomfortable conversation to try and save it, even if you don't see eye-to-eye.*

3. **Fear of failure**

   The situation: You know you need to start posting on social media more so you can spread awareness about your new candle-making business. Your friends and family have been asking you to create an Instagram profile so that they can support your business, but you're afraid of stepping onto this social platform in this capacity (you don't even know what an Instagram reel is!). Your ego taps in.

   The ego's story: *Candles won't sell on Instagram. You'll just be wasting your time. Your girlfriends won't get it. Maybe if they had businesses of their own, they would understand.*

   A better story: *Put yourself out there and stop being afraid.*

Those who love and care for you will support you regardless of what others think.

4. **Fear of success**

    The situation: You've been offered a promotion at work and the position comes with a better salary and more responsibility. The new position requires travel (which you've been begging your boss for more of) and happens to be your dream role, but you start to fear it's too good to be true.

    The ego's story: *Say no. It sounds too good to be true. There must be a catch. You don't have the time for it anyway.*

    A better story: *Take a chance on your dream. If it turns out not to be a reality, you can always pivot.*

Sometimes, we need the protection our ego can provide. If your life is in danger, by all means, listen to that ego! But if you're leaning into the ego's comfortable, muscly arms because you're scared of confronting fear, then you're wandering dangerously close to pitfall territory. It's essential to detach from the self-sabotaging ego when stepping into your storytelling power because ego shifts our ability to express ourselves consistently. You might be able to complete steps one through four and get your story out into the world, but the second you come up against a fear-shaped speedbump, your ego sidekick will jump right in, disrupting future progress unless you tell it to pipe down.

In order to detach from ego, you have to be able to identify when it is driving you. Anytime you are storytelling, whether in a conversation with a date or in a meeting with your boss, and you catch yourself expressing or reacting from a place of fear, it's likely that ego is the one speaking. Acknowledge this, be aware of its presence and recognise when it's controlling your thoughts and actions.

The more you do this, the better you'll get at noticing the thoughts or emotions that flare up your ego. Take note of these thoughts and then explore their origin. I like to do this by setting aside a dedicated moment each day to reflect on my thoughts and emotions, aiming to identify and acknowledge any instances where my ego hindered my self-expression. Once located, I then respond to it with self-compassion and replace it with a more positive thought or affirmation. The more I practice this, the easier it is for me to spot my inner fighter (and others'), and then calm it. When you take a moment to detach from your ego, you'll still be able to witness it, you just won't be as affected by it, and you won't let it call the shots anymore. You'll no longer allow ego to speak for you.

Learning how to ask the ego to take a back seat is a journey, and we all fall into this pit occasionally. Whenever I notice that I've stumbled into an ego-shaped hole, I acknowledge it by saying, 'Hello ego, thank you for protecting me, but I'm fine to continue expressing myself.' Something about this simple statement helps me leave ego behind and carry on, despite my fear. It's as if it replies, 'Oh, okay. No worries, Janika. You get back to it, then.'

Storyteller session 16:
Acknowledging the ego

Answer the following questions so you can get to know your ego, and get better at spotting it in the wild.

1. Which situations tend to bring out my ego?
2. How can I differentiate between my ego and my true self?
3. Can I think of a time my ego caused me to act in a way that did not align with my values?
4. How do I react when someone challenges my sense of self? What fear(s) come up for me?
5. What negative consequences have I experienced as a result of giving my ego too much of a say?

Use the insights from this session to reveal how your ego may be disrupting your self-expression. Remember, the more you practice identifying and acknowledging when ego takes hold, the better you'll become anticipating situations that might bring it out to play.

Pitfall 2: Comparing your story with someone else's

Are you familiar with the expression, *Comparison is the thief of joy*? Well, it's true, which is why comparison is our second pitfall. This one is a biggie, not to mention tricky. It's often disguised as 'motivation' or 'competitiveness'. Like ego, it can also sabotage opportunities and rob you of delight on your path.

In the context of storytelling, this pitfall rears its ugly head when we start comparing the way we express ourselves, our stories or achievements with those of another person. We all create our own personal stories and use self-expression to move us towards the stories we desire, but when our heads swivel to take in something another storyteller is doing – a narrative they're creating, or a way they're expressing themselves – we're bound to tumble right into this pit.

Maybe that's because we see someone on a similar path to ours achieving an outcome we'd like for ourselves. Perhaps we get trapped when another person opens our eyes to a path we didn't even know existed, and suddenly it becomes a path we desperately want to claim it as our own. Regardless of how comparison originates, once we start holding our apples next to their oranges, we're already deep in the cave of comparison. Subsequently, a trickle of inadequacy leaks into our storytelling, lowering our self-esteem and making us feel as though we're not good enough. An invisible weight settles on our shoulders as we strive to meet unattainable standards. As this pressure builds, we succumb to stress and anxiety – all while being completely distracted from our own goals and progress.

Instead of celebrating and honouring the depth of our own story, we breed resentment and jealousy around stories that aren't meant for us. We're blind to our own joy while we're in the pitfall of comparison. So, what's the answer? How can you avoid the inevitable trap of comparing your form of expression and narratives with other people's? Simple! Purely by accepting that it's normal to compare.

As humans, we're wired to be genuinely interested in what our fellow humans are doing. It's natural to have an urge to peek over the fence to check out the neighbour's grass. The key to not falling victim to comparison is to catch ourselves as we're doing this, and then remind ourselves that, while it's fine to admire and perhaps even be curious about what kind of fertiliser they're using, the second we feel that grip of envy, it's time to go back to tending to our own grass. If we don't, we're likely to get caught up chasing stories that aren't designed for us and miss the incredible potential of our own narratives.

This particular pitfall took me a little while to identify because I masked it by thinking, I'm just competitive. I'd see someone doing something I admired or found interesting and would immediately start placing their life story next to mine – holding the fabric of mine up to the light to see where the holes were, even though my story was spun from completely different material to theirs.

At first, it was challenging to put myself on social media and start talking about the power of storytelling. There were 400 people following my Instagram profile, and they came from various pockets of my life. I hadn't posted much in years, so most of these followers knew me from my high school and university days. They had no knowledge into the story I'd been writing for myself throughout my mid-to-late twenties. As I began emerging from the content closet, and shyly uploading posts about the importance of personal storytelling or the benefits of reviewing the narrative within to live an aligned life, the response from these followers was . . . Well, crickets. They didn't know what the heck I was talking about, and they definitely didn't understand how important storytelling was to personal development.

Around this same time, a friend of mine embarked on a new chapter in her life. She was growing a cosmetic injectables business and creating social media content to reach her target market. Over scrambled eggs at a café one morning, we bonded over the ups and downs of wrangling Instagram reels, and the challenges of algorithms or gaining new followers. A few days later, I made the mistake of going to her page to compare her follower count with mine. Before I knew it, I'd fallen into a comparison pit.

Week by week, her followers continued to increase while (at times) mine decreased! I couldn't understand it. I continued to compare our progress, and be frustrated by the gap in our metrics. It wasn't until I took a step back, put down my phone and made an effort to revisit and reconnect to my reason for engaging with social media in the first place that I started to climb out of this pit. I realised it was inevitable that we'd progress at different rates; my friend was posting about famous people's lips and how to hide wrinkles, while I was posting about connecting to your true self and how looking within can lead to your true narrative. One of these topics is way easier to digest on a social platform, and I can tell ya, it ain't soul storytelling! After this moment of clarity, the lens of comparison was lifted.

Today, I view my stumble as an innocent and highly relatable example of how quickly comparison can swallow our storytelling power. Instead of focusing on the story I wanted to tell and building a community of followers who connected with my message, I was focusing on my friend's followers and her journey. My problem wasn't that I was competing with her for likes and follows; it was that I wasn't honouring my own storytelling because I was too busy trying to match hers. I never viewed her success in the same competitive light after this. Instead, I accepted that although we were both on the same platform, we were telling completely different stories on different paths using different skills.

Acceptance and integration of our own personal story and self-expression are the keys to unlocking freedom and detouring around comparison so you can carry on attracting what is designed for you. My five storytelling steps won't miraculously turn you into the best storyteller of all time, but they will turn you into the best storyteller of *your* story. The journey is about becoming who you were always meant to be through your self-expression – even if it's a slow burn. It's about taking responsibility, having moments of self-realisation and being self-aware. Understanding exactly who you are, what has meaning to you, and what drives you is precisely what gives you permission to share all of those things with the world. When you have this level of self-awareness, comparison becomes irrelevant.

Pitfall 3: Feeling like an impostor in your own narrative

From the ages of 14 to 17, the image of Jessica Alba's washboard abs greeted me every morning when I opened my eyes. I'd been a diehard fan since watching her dance her way through *Honey*, one of my favourite movies of the early 2000s. Remember, dancing was my passion, and Alba's brown skin and gyrating hips entered my consciousness while I was navigating puberty as a non-white female. I adored her.

After devouring an interview with her in *Dolly* magazine, I cut her image out and slapped it on my wall as a reminder that brown girls ruled (and could also dance). A quote from the interview was printed next to her picture: 'Even if you don't know what you're doing, fake it till you make it.' Those words of advice resonated with me, especially later.

When I became a young model, I found myself in environments with no idea of what the hell I was supposed to be doing. People would just shout, 'Walk here, then exit stage left,' or 'Fly there and smile,' and I was expected to get on with it. I'd get pushed down runways in heels that were too big for me, and while walking towards the cameras and praying I wouldn't fall, I'd think: *Be like Jessica Alba*. I'd repeat this over and over as a way to remind myself to pretend I was confident until I was safely back behind the curtain again. This worked (sort of), but, the thing about pretending is that it only gets you so far. Before you know it, you start feeling unworthy of being there, and the narrative of being an imposter becomes another pitfall we have to avoid.

During this period in my life, I found myself deeply engrossed in playing the role of someone who was completely immersed in the glamorous world of fashion. However, deep down I carried a sense of unworthiness that clashed with my surroundings. Instead of embracing my unique journey and showcasing that story, I wasted precious moments engulfed in feelings of inadequacy.

In a full-circle moment, I recently heard Jessica Alba talk openly on Jay Shetty's podcast about her experiences of suffering from impostor syndrome. Turns out she speaks often of how she felt undeserving of success when she transitioned from Hollywood actress to entrepreneur. Proof that even celebrities fall into this storyteller pitfall from time to time –probably while they're portraying the very characters that inspire us!

We know imposter syndrome can swallow up our ability to showcase our storytelling, but what exactly is this 'syndrome'? Best described as a psychological phenomenon, it's when we start to doubt our abilities even though we are more than capable. This prompts a sinking fear that we'll be 'exposed' as a fraud, and we can experience this regardless of whether those feelings of incompetence have any merit. While we're in this imposter pit, we struggle with self-doubt, feelings of inadequacy and a sense of being unworthy of our achievements and success. We feel as though we're faking it, even when we have evidence to the contrary.

If you've ever attributed your success to chance, dumb luck or an external factor that had absolutely nothing to do with your hard work or skill, you are familiar with impostor syndrome. It's unbelievably common to feel this way, yet it wasn't something that was openly discussed until fairly recently, despite so many people – including those at the very top of their game – experiencing it at some point. When the fear you'll be exposed as a fake creeps in, or a deep-rooted sense of inadequacy stops you from expressing your story altogether, you're stuck in this pitfall, and it's time to get out.

At some point, most of us will fall into this trap of not feeling good enough, ready enough or perfect enough, and if we stay there, we will never have the confidence to share a story. If we consistently surrender to feeling unworthy of our narratives and their ability to carry our self-expressions in them, there won't be any storytellers left! If Jessica Alba feels that way, what hope is there for us mere mortals? This, my friends, is the ladder you need to crawl out of this pitfall: the knowledge that *everybody*, including leaders of countries, Nobel laureates, founders of billion-dollar corporations and A-list celebrities all deal with imposter syndrome. The way out of this pitfall is to identify the stories that only you bring to the table, and acknowledge all the reasons you are worthy of sharing your voice. Then, you can proudly accept that you are deserving of expressing yourself, and that you do have a story worthy of listening to.

Pitfall 4: Allowing your voice to be silenced

We're at the fifth and final pitfall, and to be honest with you, once again this last one has been the most challenging one for me to write. Depending on where you're at on this storytelling journey, the truth I'm about to share with you might be hard to digest, but here goes: I genuinely believe that we are all equal. Every fibre in my being understands that my neighbour is just as worthy of expressing their story as I am of expressing mine. The *reality*, however, is that our society does not support equality in storytelling.

Not all voices are treated the same, and no matter how much we might want to buy into the illusion that there's a level playing field or we live in a just and fair world, the fact of the matter is that we, as a collective, place a higher value on stories expressed by certain storytellers. Usually, the storyteller's race, gender, background, education and wealth dictates how valued their story is, but many other factors such as class, age, religion, sexual orientation, disability, weight, neurology and nationality also influence this. Whichever metric is used, one thing is certain: the storyteller who is valued is likely to have their story broadcast the loudest, too. This is storytelling privilege, and voices that have this privilege are often given bigger platforms and louder microphones than other storytellers present in the same scenario. Period.

The problem with championing certain voices, is that other voices – especially those offering perspectives or opinions that challenge or contradict those of the privileged storytellers – are silenced. This version of censorship keeps dissenting voices quiet while turning up the volume on the most 'valued' stories. I'm not here to argue how damaging this can be, I'm simply pointing out that's it's something that exists. Hopefully, being aware of it will help you identify when storytelling privilege is being used to silence others so you can move around it. This is a pitfall you will likely find yourself in multiple times. I certainly have.

An interesting thing I discovered about storytelling privilege is that it isn't universal, and by that, I mean having privilege in some spaces doesn't protect you from being silenced in others because it's subjective. Whether or not your voice and story will be valued depends heavily on the spaces you're expressing yourself in, and the values of the people receiving your story. Each of us has certain advantages or entitlements that will benefit us in some arenas and count against us in others.

It's also worth noting that even if you're privileged in most regards, you can still be silenced from sharing your story. Most people have a memory of having their voice snuffed or not being given a fair chance to be heard. Let's break down a few tactics commonly used to muzzle a storyteller.

Marginalising: Limiting a person/group's ability to be heard by ignoring them or relying on systemic oppression or existing discrimination of whichever group they belong to. Typically, marginalised communities such as people of colour, LGBTQ+ individuals, and people with disabilities experience this type of silencing.

Censorship: Occurs when a powerful entity (such as government or military) exercises control over access to information and platforms, preventing others from freely expressing themselves. Countries with dictatorships often experience this type of restricted access to freedom of speech.

De-platforming: Preventing access to platforms or opportunities to share a story is a type of silencing. An excellent example of this is when an anti-government radio station is shut down in a dictatorship.

Intimidation: When a person or group is coerced, or threatened with acts of violence or harassed with fear tactics, they may be forced to swallow their self-expression because of fear.

Societal pressure: Sometimes, political/cultural/social climates cause people to fear the consequences of sharing their truth because the current environment is unsafe to do so. They may be fearful of facing legal repercussions or violence, or of losing their income or being ostracised and discriminated against.

Gaslighting: Tricking someone into doubting their own experiences, opinions or memories by contradicting their experiences is known as gaslighting. This forces a person to stay silent because it makes them question the validity of their story and wonder if others will believe them.

On a red-eye flight from New York to Los Angeles, I experienced the silencing tactic of marginalisation. I often end up chatting with the person next to me on a plane because to pass the time, so I always pray I get seated next to an interesting person. On this flight, my prayers were answered, and I was next to a lovely girl about my age with big green eyes and pale skin. Within minutes, we were happily chatting about our adventures in New York City.

Partway through our conversation, I noticed the flight attendant making her way down the aisle with the drinks trolley. When she reached our row, I expected her to ask me first since I was in the aisle seat. 'Ma'am,' she asked, 'what would you like to drink?' I started to answer, only she wasn't looking at me; she was looking at my new friend, who promptly ordered a Coke. *Strange*, I thought. The flight attendant repeated the question, and as I opened my mouth again, I realised her eyes still weren't on me. This time, she was speaking to the older white woman by the window. *Maybe she serves the drinks in a weird order*, I thought as she passed the woman her drink. But when she pushed the trolley right past me, I realised she wasn't planning on serving me at all.

'Excuse me!' I said, turning around. I knew the flight attendant could hear me, but she didn't turn around. As she continued serving drinks, it dawned on me that I was being silenced. I deserved a drink as much as my friendly neighbour did, but this woman wasn't interested in hearing me or taking my order. I got up and walked towards her, raising my voice a little louder. 'Hey!' I said, 'You missed me. Can I please get a Sprite?' She looked at me and quickly made an BS excuse for treating me differently to my neighbours: 'Oh!' She exclaimed. 'I thought you'd speak Spanish, and I don't speak it, so I figured I wouldn't bother trying.' She shoved a Sprite at me, turned around and kept going. Upon reflection, I realised that the flight attendant had tried to silence me by ignoring me. In her eyes, my voice didn't hold the same weight as the two women sitting with me. In some situations, I have come to realise that I will not be heard for no other reason than the person doesn't value my voice. Armed with this truth, I can now prepare myself for that sinking feeling in my heart, and I've learned to not surrender to it by speaking with power, and standing tall in the certainty that my voice is just as worthy. If we don't back ourselves in moments of silencing, no one else will.

There are no perfect solutions because we don't live in a perfect world. Pitfalls exist for all of us, and the faster you learn to recognise them, the quicker you'll be able to climb out of them. Stand up, and ask for your Sprite.

Applying step 5 in real life

Now that you're familiar with these pitfalls, I want to show you how avoiding them will help you harness the power of your narratives in everyday situations. Accepting that these pitfalls will continue to challenge us and finding the confidence to escape them are crucial to expressing yourself authentically, which is what's required if you want to step into your storytelling power completely. You've got to show up with your voice and stand tall, even if you stumble. This time, I'm going to give you examples of particular pitfalls in action, then provide you with a simple mantra you can use to help you conquer that particular storytelling pitfall should you find yourself in facing it.

WORK

Navigating a storytelling pitfall at work can lead to feelings of being overlooked, demotivated, and dissatisfied. Although these challenges may arise, it is crucial to overcome them in order to truly express yourself within the workplace.

Exit the ego

Acknowledging when you're struggling with your ego can assist you in recalibrating your mindset to better serve your core intention and messaging. This mindfulness helps you remain conscious of how you're coming across to your audience so that you can continue building positive and respectful relationships with coworkers while still communicating your message.

Real-life application: There are company cutbacks looming and you are scared your job might be on the line. Your ego taps in, and you start bragging about your achievements whenever your boss is in earshot. You also dismiss the efforts of others, which diminishes your audience's desire to listen to you or collaborate.

Mantra: *My ego does not control my actions.*

Cancelling colleague comparison

When we are struggling to keep up or feeling that our work is not quite good enough compared with our colleagues or competitors, we might throw a self-sabotaging spanner in our own efforts. The demotivating emotions of anxiety and insecurity creep into our working environments, and we might find we struggle to express our own progress and accomplishments even more than before.

Real-life application: Understand that focusing too much on others' achievements and comparing them with your own is detrimental to your growth and development because it makes you less likely to want to share your performance with the team.

Mantra: *We are all writing our own individual stories.*

Fire your imposter syndrome

Doubting our own abilities because we're terrified to be seen as not knowing what we're doing in our workspace can swallow our expression whole. When we suffer from imposter syndrome, we don't feel comfortable sharing our voice and will hesitate to progress in our careers. Even if we have the necessary skills and experiences, we can still remain trapped in the same chapter of life if we don't continue our narrative.

Real-life application: If you're promoted (because you are the best and most skilled candidate, but fall into the trap of thinking that you're not qualified or capable enough to do the job, you will continue to minimise your accomplishments, hesitate to make decisions or take on new responsibilities and stop communicating your capabilities to the decision makers who need to see it.

Mantra: *I have unique talents, skills, stories and narratives that make me valuable to this role.*

Slaying silencing

Being silenced in the workplace can lead to feelings of powerlessness, fear of consequences and feeling undervalued. All of these can decrease our motivation and contribute to a toxic work environment that results in your voice not being heard, even when you do communicate.

Real-life application: A supervisor or manager you report to micromanages you to the point where you feel undervalued and like your voice is neither heard nor valued. You're terrified to bring this to the attention of your top-tier management in case there are consequences, so you say nothing at all and remain silent in a job that is damaging your well-being.

Mantra: *My voice deserves to be heard and valued, and I respect myself enough to speak up.*

RELATIONSHIPS

In the context of relationships, if a storyteller is stuck in one or more of these four pitfalls and has no intention of leaving them, it's safe to assume the relationship is not healthy. We must be conscious enough to accept that all of us occasionally filter a story through the lens of one, if not more, pitfalls. Being aware of this and communicating this to our friend, partner or family member helps us connect to that person in a way that is honest and raw, and furthers the chances that they will accurately interpret our intended expression.

Choose empathy over ego
When we prioritise our own ego in conversations with people we have a relationship with, we are sending them the message that we prioritise our sense of self above a sense of fairness and reality. They will not hear our message if it's being drowned out by our ego saying, 'I'm more important than you.'

Real-life application: Your partner tells you they'd like to spend more time with you this week, and you immediately shut the idea down because you're fearful that you won't have enough time to finish all the work your boss has given you. Letting ego step in, you word vomit to that you're way too busy and that it's not your fault they have nothing else going on in their own life. Understandably, they are hurt and leave the house in anger. Had you responded more empathetically, you would have discovered that they'd had some sad news from home this week. Asking for more time with you was their way of communicating they needed support and some cheering up. It's likely this revelation would have deepened your connection, but instead, ego has fractured it.

Mantra: *Let my love speak before my ego.*

Caught up comparing

Comparing yourself or your story to someone you're in a relationship with can make you feel inadequate or like you're not meeting society's standards, or perhaps the other person's expectations of you. The sense of doubt this type of comparison causes can lead to jealousy, insecurity and harmful thinking. Being caught up in this comparison gives us tunnel vision in the wrong direction. Instead of prioritising our own stories, we get stuck in someone else's.

Real-life application: Comparing your timeline with a friend who has recently experienced a life-changing event, such as starting a new job, having a baby or getting engaged. If you're not at that life stage (and would like to be), you can get caught up comparing your story where you shouldn't and neglect your own narrative.

Mantra: *There is no race in this story I'm creating.*

She's an imposter

Feelings of not belonging or not being good enough can fester into an awkward sense of inauthenticity. When you communicate from this place, those around you are likely to pick up on it and not take your word at face value.

Real-life application: Attempting to integrate into a new group of friends and feeling not good enough causes you to express opinions and share stories that are not true and authentic to you. Eventually, these new friends will pick up on this and come to distrust your storytelling.

Mantra: *Every day I show up exactly as I am.*

Silence no more

If you feel uncomfortable expressing yourself in a relationship, it is time to remove those inhibitions and express yourself freely. The other person may be silencing you intentionally or unintentionally, but regardless, once you start speaking your true narrative, those who are meant to be in your life will remain, and those who are not will have to leave and make room for the new.

Real-life application: Following an argument with your partner where they didn't give you a chance to share your perspective, you try to express your feelings to them, but instead of listening, they interrupt you and say you're too emotional before changing the subject completely. You start to feel like your emotions and concerns are not valued or important, and this leads to resentment and frustration.

Mantra: *The people who are good for me will support my voice.*

SELF

We can be our own worst enemy, and when we fall into a pitfall, sometimes the only person keeping us in there is ourself.

Self-talk ego

When the ego starts to spiral, it can take you down with it. It may not be expressing its thoughts out loud for an audience, but if you allow it to run the show internally by narrating thoughts of entitlement, superiority or self-importance, this will negatively affect your mental health and wellbeing.

Real-life application: If we don't get invited to an event we expected to be invited to, our egocentric mind may kick in. We may start replaying our interactions with those involved and start creating narratives that don't exist to support our ego's story. We waste time focusing on issues that likely don't even exist.

Mantra: *I can only control my own actions and story.*

Mirror mirror

We've all played the endless comparison game of staring in the mirror and wishing our eyebrows were a little thicker, or our waist was narrower like that influencer on social media. All this does is lead to feelings of inadequacy and disappointment with our own stories. It's so important to notice when you are falling into this pitfall. Be really mindful of how you're talking to yourself when you're alone.

Real-life application: While getting ready for work, you start comparing yourself to someone you follow on social media. While thinking of their glamorous photos, you start to feel frumpy and underdressed. And though you spent 20 minutes doing your hair, you now decide you hate it, so you pull it out and start again.

Mantra: *My self-worth comes from honouring my unique story.*

Inadequate inside

The internal dialogue we have with ourselves all day, every day can be challenging if it's laced with thoughts that consistently focus on how we're an imposter who is fooling everyone. This 'I'm not good enough' story will hinder your ability to move forward and go for what you want, even when you thoroughly deserve it.

Real-life application: A friend brings you along to her weekly running group, which you've been dying to join for months because they are all training for the marathon you want to run. While introducing you, your friend talks up all the medals you've been winning for running. Even though you're passionate about this new hobby and have been training hard, you shrug her praise off uncomfortably while telling yourself and everyone else that these accomplishments are all down to luck. You are sure these experienced runners will see through you, and consider making an excuse and leaving. You don't feel worthy of your marathon goals, and this diminishes your ability to confidently make a good impression and go after what you desire.

Mantra: *My achievements and failures have prepared me for this chapter.*

Self-silencing

Believe it or not, you can silence yourself if you don't, feel worthy of expressing yourself at your core. Self-censorship occurs when you disconnect from your thoughts and feelings.

Real-life application: Say you strongly believe in the urgency of addressing plastic pollution and its impact on climate change. The bad news is, you also find yourself working at a plastics factory and fearful of the consequences of losing your secured job, you continue on, suppressing your convictions. This inner struggle takes a toll on you emotionally and mentally. Witnessing the environmental harm caused by the factory's practices fills you with guilt and conflict and ignoring your values and failing to honour your expression becomes increasingly challenging. It erodes your integrity and authenticity, leading to frustration and a sense of being trapped. Acknowledging this toll is crucial. By honouring your inner expression, and seeking alternative work aligned with your beliefs, you regain integrity, purpose, and fulfillment.

Mantra: *I trust my unique voice.*

CHAPTER EIGHT

Start sharing your stories

No matter who you are or what you do, your ability to communicate through stories will determine the direction your life takes. I know I've already hammered this point throughout the book, but storytelling truly can make or break a moment. The right story told at the right time, and in the right way, can determine whether you end up on the path you want to be on. In short, your storytelling ability can alter your life as you know it. I cannot overstate the importance of being a powerful storyteller, so now it's time for you to show up as one.

Luckily for us, the storytelling mediums available to us in the modern day are vast and diverse. Gone are the days a lone gatekeeper could silence your expression. Today, you have agency over your words as long as you're able to show up and claim your authority to speak. Storytelling power is a skill that requires practice and a deep understanding of the self, the target audience and human nature. One of the questions I field the most is, 'Who's going to want to hear my story?' I love this question because the answer is 'So many people!' Some of the most powerful stories come from everyday people who've lived through an experience or learned a lesson, then decided to open up about their life.

A good story is born when a storyteller conveys a compelling narrative in a way that is specific to the needs and interests of their audience. When a story resonates, a connection forms and their message not only lands, it sticks. People assume that if they aren't famous or well-known, others won't be interested in what they have to say. But the opposite is true! Many famous people can't connect precisely because they don't relate to everyday life. Trust in the value of your experiences and ideas. As long as your story comes from a place of truth other people are bound to see themselves in it and connect to it in a meaningful way. All that's left beyond that is for you to pick the best medium for that truth to be expressed, and I'm here to help with a few suggestions.

Written word

Books

- ✓ A classical storytelling medium that offers deep immersion and engagement. With many different genres available to best suit your expression, you can choose to self-publish or go down the traditional route of publishing to bring their stories to life best.
- ✗ Requires significant time, money and effort in a highly competitive environment. There is also gatekeeping if you plan on traditionally publishing (i.e., writing a book that a

publishing house will have to accept, print and distribute on your behalf), not to mention the chance of rejection. There's also often a long time between writing the book and getting to the customer, so you might find the cultural conversation has shifted by the time your book is published.

Articles

- ✓ This is a significantly faster way to express yourself, and a particularly useful for informing, educating or motivating a reader.

- ✗ Moving past the gatekeepers can be challenging. There may also be a limited audience if the publication or outlet publishing your article is niche. Finding the right balance between storytelling and informing can also be challenging.

Blog posts

- ✓ Publishing a story online means opening the opportunity for it to be discovered and shared by people worldwide. Publishing instantly also means you are able to speak on something in the moment it's relevant and happening.

- ✗ It can be frightening to detail personal experiences and stories online for anyone to read, share and comment on.

Spoken word

Theatre

- ✓ An immersive experience that can even incorporate all storytelling mediums into one. It creates a level of intimacy and shared community that is hugely impactful, and hard to recreate through other mediums.

✗ Time- and cost-consuming, requires significant resources and logistical planning to help bring your story to life. Also involves relying on multiple other people to help bring your vision to life, which may get lost in translation.

Conversations

✓ The oldest, most familiar and direct way sharing a story that is easily accessible and instant. It provides real-time feedback from the audience through conversation and shared dialogue.

✗ Can be interrupted, disrupting the storytelling flow.

Podcasts

✓ A sense of intimacy between the audience and storyteller can be created through long-form conversation, and it's very accessible, and can be either read (via transcription) or listened to wherever you are, and during whatever you're doing.

✗ It can be challenging to create a theme compelling enough to structure a podcast around and hold the attention of an audience week after week because, unlike video, they are only accessing audio.

Visual

Films

✓ Extremely immersive because of its ability to combine multiple modes of storytelling. In addition, the use of film techniques such as lighting, angles and design can work together to add atmosphere and emotion to the story.

- ✗ Equipment and entire process is costly, not to mention time-consuming to produce. Need specialist team to bring it together.

Art
- ✓ Visual art, sculpture, music and dance can convey complex emotions and topics that may be difficult to express through words.

- ✗ Because of the highly subjective nature of these mediums, not every audience will interpret your message and intention the way you intend.

Branding
- ✓ When done well, a brand can engage customers. When a customer identifies with a brand, they are more likely to feel a sense of loyalty towards that company, service or product.

- ✗ Relying too heavily on a brand to tell a story can dilute the impact a product or service has by not allowing it to speak for itself.

Social media

Meta (formerly Facebook)
- ✓ Combining storytelling efforts across Instagram and Facebook is seamless and offers an opportunity to reach a lot of people. These platforms are highly accessible, and anyone with a

phone can create an account and upload content from (almost) anywhere in the world, for free. Paid advertising can also be incorporated to assist in building a direct connection to a particular audience.

✗ Censorship can stop you from communicating your story as you envision (for example, images of the female nipple and certain terms are often censored on this platform).

YouTube

✓ Because this platform is owned by the biggest search engine in the world, sharing your story in this mode can assist you in reaching the greatest number of people. Similarly to Meta, accessibility is a big plus because you can upload content for free, instantly.

✗ It's time-consuming to create long-form videos and consistently show up, and you're at the mercy of the platform's algorithm when it comes to how many people your video will be shown to.

TikTok

✓ Because the platform only sometimes prioritises creators with established followers and accounts, it makes it possible for someone with no following to go viral with a story.

✗ As one of the newer social platforms, TikTok continues to face controversy over visibility and the accusation of data collection and is not available in every country.

Which medium you choose will depend on the story you are sharing and the form of self-expression that comes most naturally to you. Not every story is suited to every medium. As the sole authority on your stories, it's up to you to judge how best to express your storytelling power.

Progress, not perfection

Some quotes stay with me forever – likely because they elegantly and succinctly sum up a story or feeling I relate to. Or perhaps they stay with me because a great quote that is simple, and easy to remember (and quote back) can hide a surprising amount of depth. I don't recall where I was when I first heard Gabby Bernstein talk for the first time, but I know that I felt a light go on in me when I heard her say the words, 'Progress, not perfection.' The bestselling author, international speaker and motivational new age thinker bridges the gap between spirituality, modern wellness and inner expression with such a captivating and honest voice.

I admire Gabby's dedication to her beliefs and desire to speak her heart's truth with the goal of helping others to do the same. People (and by 'people' I mean her community of hundreds of thousands) say the universe brings Gabby to you when you need to hear her, and that was certainly true for me. I was on the verge of spreading my wings, about to leave my corporate job to step into my new career as a storyteller guide.

I needed a Gabby in my life because I had big, fat non-conventional dreams and was stuck like glue to my fear. I was desperate for conditions to be perfect before I attempted to fully express myself. After digesting every podcast/book/talk she had available, she said those three little words that, when strung together, pushed me off the cliff of fear and forced me to start flapping my wings: 'Progress, not perfection.'

This quote is a response to the way we can get so hung up on perfection that we don't make any progress at all. We wait for conditions to be just right before starting anything new, or we get stuck in the trap of perfectionism and say things like, 'I'll do it when this happens.' 'I'll start once I have more of that.' 'I'll know it when I see it.' Or, 'I'll wait until they ask me.' These narratives keep us stuck, and keep us from achieving our dreams. The broom of fear sweeps us up while we're waiting for all of the answers to find us. We hold out for a state of perfection before attempting to connect with our story, and stay stagnant instead of sharing our voice or moving forward. Because of this, we miss our chance. We miss the opportunity. We miss the story.

Perfectionism can also create unrealistic expectations that lead to an ongoing issue of procrastination and inaction because instead of attempting to work towards the story we desire, we get caught up in small details and become overwhelmed by one of the fears we covered in chapter five. It's okay for us to acknowledge that we won't always feel ready to express ourselves or share our stories. It's when we show up in spite of this that the magic happens. Small, incremental movements open doors to opportunity and can create the story we desire. And if we make mistakes, well, that's okay, too. They are a natural part of life and the things that provide us with valuable learnings – the gems that can be used to shape our future stories.

You may feel the urge to hide behind a wall of perfectionism before expressing your story. Perhaps you are hesitating because you haven't figured everything out. Maybe you feel that the narrative isn't perfect yet, or you don't have all the answers. But it's important to remember that sharing your story with power is not about being perfect; it's about being your true self in its most powerful form. Your voice is unique and valuable – it's not supposed to be perfect!

When you share your story, you have the power to inspire others, build connections, and steer the direction of your life. The more you practice showing up in your storytelling power, the more comfortable you will feel in the role of storyteller. As you see the progress you've made and the positive effect storytelling has on your life, you'll wonder why you didn't start earlier!

Keep the below tips in mind whenever you need a reminder to kick perfectionism to the curb so you can realign with a mindset of progress.

- **Embrace failure:** Don't fear the big F-word. It's okay to fail. We're human, not AI. Each one of our mistakes is an opportunity to learn, improve or help us connect with others.

- **Celebrate progress:** Focus on how far you've come and be sure to celebrate your successes. Celebrating even the smallest of story-wins and using that as motivation to keep going is essential.

- **Find your people:** This is a big one. Surround yourself with people who believe in you and appreciate your voice. They can help keep you accountable and remind you to keep going when you need encouragement.

- **Practice self-compassion:** You have to be kind to yourself because this is a long journey. Remember, you're doing the best with what you have. Mastering any skill takes time.

- **Continue to take imperfect action:** In keeping with the 'Progress, not perfection' theme, I encourage you to keep going no matter what. Imperfect action is better than no action at all.

A mindset of progress, not perfection, will keep you going along your desired path and help you to continue using your storytelling power as you focus on moving forward, taking action and learning lessons along the way.

Become a force in the world

With the five steps in your arsenal, the next question becomes, what will you do with your storytelling power? How will you use it to shape your narrative in this book of life and elevate you from character to creator? By claiming this power, you will change your life, and also the lives of others because stepping into your storytelling power will help the people around you to do the same, or, at the very least, help them see themselves and their narratives reflected in your sincere expression.

The more you draw upon this inner power, the easier it will become to summon it to the surface in any scenario. As with the start of a fitness journey, strengthening a muscle and improving your overall fitness can feel daunting, especially when trying machinery and tools you've not used often – but if you continue showing up to work out every day, gradually, these tools will become familiar. You'll begin noticing that you can easily recall exercises and routines, and you'll definitely start noticing your body changing. You'll get stronger, and then exercising will no longer be a chore; it will be something you enjoy, and something you want to keep doing because it makes you feel good, and doing it is now second nature.

With great force and power comes great responsibility. It is important to use your storytelling power with integrity because stories can significantly impact the people we express them to. If your stories come from a good place, you can continue sending out a high vibration, and attracting a similar vibration back to you. Even if the contents of your story are not positive or good, as long as it is expressed from this higher vibration, good can still come from it. For example, social change, raising awareness or inspiring a community to take action can be the result of telling stories of social injustices.

Storytelling for a greater good doesn't need to be done at that macro level, either. (Not all of us are trying to change the world.) You may prefer to use your storytelling power at the micro level, and express yourself to a smaller audience in order to improve your wellbeing. This might look like talking to a therapist in order to overcome inner trauma, or becoming clear with yourself about your priority purpose. Whichever level you aim your story at, ensure you're always speaking from the heart. That way, you'll hit the audience strong when using your storytelling power because your words, thoughts and expressions will hold serious weight, even when you can't see it.

Your words are more powerful than you might think

Dr Masaru Emoto, a Japanese author and researcher gained international recognition for his work studying the relationship between water and human consciousness. His most famous book, *The Hidden Messages in Water*, which sold millions of copies, focused on the idea that thoughts, words and emotions could directly impact molecular structures.

Emoto wanted to demonstrate that words have the power to affect our physical world and personal health. Using high-speed photography, he exposed water to various stimuli, including words, thoughts and music. Immediately afterwards, he'd freeze it and then observe it under a microscope. When he looked closely, he noticed that the crystalline structure changed depending on which specific, concentrated thoughts it had been exposed to.

Water exposed to loving, kind and positive words and stimuli would form beautiful and intricate crystal snowflake patterns. In comparison, water exposed to negative thoughts and hateful comments formed chaotic, ununified, incomplete patterns. I'm not kidding when I say you should put this book down and Google the images from this experiment. They are fascinating to look at!

Perhaps you've heard of other variations on this phenomenon. Ever had a friend or family member with a green thumb tell you to speak lovingly to your plants? It's a real thing! I was gifted a house plant after a big move, and it has always been one of my favourites. It's hard to kill and easy to love, and whenever I notice that he (yes, this plant is a 'he') is drooping and looks sad, I give him some water and whisper sweet nothings to him. The next day, he's standing upright, proud, green and happy. It's probably the water, but I like to think my words help, too. A while back, I figured if this worked for the plant, maybe it would work for me, too. I started whispering kind nothings to myself when I was in the shower, and guess what, this actually does work for me on days I feel rather droopy!

If you want to try these theories out for yourself, you can recreate Dr Emoto's 'rice experiment'. Place three jars of cooked rice in a room and speak to the jars every day for a month. The first jar gets lots of nice positive words (e.g., thank you or love). The second jar gets only negative words (e.g., disgusting or hate), and the third jar should be ignored completely.

If your results are the same as Dr Emoto's, by the end of the month, the rice in the first jar should be in the best condition and have the least amount of mold growing on it. The third jar (the one you ignored), will probably have a bit of mold, and the rice in the second jar (the one you were mean to) will likely be in the worst condition and be growing the most mold. Emoto concluded that positive and negative words and thoughts can affect the molecular structure of water and, therefore, our physical reality, which is hugely interesting when you consider our human bodies are made up of approximately 60 per cent water.

The life-altering impact of stories

I promised I would show you how storytelling could change your life with practical examples, so let's do that now. If you aren't yet convinced, then this is our last chance to drill down on this and make sure you close this book with no more doubts by looking at four main takeaways.

Work

1. **Create a memorable brand**

    A well-crafted story will solidify and enhance your brand's awareness by making it more memorable, sharable and engaging.

2. **Communicate values**

    A compelling narrative can showcase shared values and experiences, helping you to connect with customers, colleagues, and employees on a deeper level.

3. **Inspire action**

    Powerful stories can drive a particular outcome by inspiring or motivating people internally and externally.

4. **Provide context**

    Storytelling can assist in connection to complex ideas and make them more understandable, relatable and actionable.

Relationships

1. **Increase understanding**

   A powerful story shared from your perspective can help others understand where you're coming from, even if they haven't been through the same thing or disagree with your point of view.

2. **Create shared experiences**

   When you tell a story that involves multiple people, it can help deepen intimacy and create collective stories.

3. **Strengthen bonds**

   Similarly, when you open up and share a meaningful story, it shows you trust the listener to reveal that part of yourself, deepening your bond.

4. **Facilitate problem-solving**

   Compelling storytelling can propel your communication when an issue in a relationship needs addressing.

Self

1. **Greater resilience**

   Knowing what your story is, is a journey in itself. Using your storytelling power to focus on the positive aspects of the experience, even in the face of adversity, can help you gain a sense of control in your life.

2. **Build a sense of purpose**
   Sharing your story (even just with yourself) can help you gain a sense of purpose and meaning.

3. **Improved mental health**
   Expressing yourself can help relieve mental health struggles like anxiety or depression. By sharing difficult experiences, we can find common ground with others who have also experienced these to reduce our feelings of isolation.

4. **Increase self-awareness**
   Storytelling can help you reflect on your experiences, emotions and thoughts, leading to a greater sense of self-understanding.

Our words hold life-altering power, so it's so essential we remember to use our new force for good. Empower and lift up the voices of others by setting an example of how to contribute to a more positive and sustainable future for all through the power of storytelling.

You've got the force

As natural storytellers wired for expression, stories are how we share our experiences, communicate our essence and make sense of the world around us. But, as I've suggested, storytelling isn't just a way for us to entertain and connect with one another, it is also a powerful tool we can use to achieve our goals and help us live the life we desire. After all, each of us is creating our life's story in this very moment, and whether we realise it or not it's the most important book on our bookshelf.

When we tell a story with this power behind us, we can influence others to see things from our perspective, connect with our journey and take action in the direction we favour. When you examine what happens when you don't tell a story powerfully, it's obvious how essential it is. Even so, it's easy to become disconnected from our inner narratives and risk expressing ourselves poorly or inaccurately. So, the question is, do we write our life story with determination and strength, even when it's challenging to do so? Or do we write it timidly, with a frail and shaky hand? Do we hand the pen to others we consider stronger to craft our story for us?

You now know the answer to this question and have the information to access this strength within yourself. With your knowledge of the 5 Steps to Storytelling Power, you can recharge your own battery and activate your expression from within as you charge towards your desired narratives. If you find yourself disconnected from these steps in the future, I encourage you to revisit this book. Go back to the step that makes you the most uncomfortable, work through the step you scoffed at again, or dive deeper into specific areas you may have glossed over. I promise you that there is a narrative inside you waiting to be examined and reclaimed.

To fully embrace and access your storytelling power, you need to embrace all five steps at the same time. Each one of the steps is a building block, and by adding them together and making one whole, you, my friend, are stepping into your storytelling power. As such, let's review them as an equation.

5 STEPS TO STORYTELLING POWER

Step 1: Making space for your narratives

+

Step 2: Knowing who you (truly) are

+

Step 3: Crafting a strong purpose

+

Step 4: Expressing yourself effectively

+

Step 5: Conquering the storytelling pitfalls

=

You stepping into your storytelling power!

The end of this equation is where you reap the benefits of all your hard work. You'll have access to a deep well of determination, resilience and creativity that can help you overcome challenges, get honest with yourself and achieve your dreams. Reconnecting with your most true and conscious self is what allows you to express your true feelings and desires, and live a life that is both authentic and meaningful to you on an individual level. The potential to transform your own life and also positively impact the world around you are very real, and I can't think of a greater story you could write than the one you connect to at that heart level. You'll need to stay connected at that heart level because taking ownership of your story requires great courage, vulnerability and self-awareness.

This story of your life is such a precious gift, and its narrative is shaped every day by the way you express yourself (both internally and externally). Regardless of your upbringing, circumstances, culture or life experience, you have the power within you to direct this uniquely personal narrative with your beliefs, attitudes, thoughts, and storytelling.

Armed with the five steps, take notice of how your storytelling interactions alter in your day-to-day life. You'll see a clear difference between the way you used to express yourself and how you show up now. Whether you're using storytelling to build relationships, enhance a business, progress your career, make sense of experiences, inspire and motivate others or simply express yourself creatively, the act of embracing your storytelling power will provide a foundational belief that you are the authority on your own story. Most importantly, though, you'll have so much more control over the story of your life, and in a chaotic and unpredictable world, that sense of inner power is more valuable than ever.

Inevitably, going on this journey will give you more insight into the people around you who are neglecting or disowning their inner power. The fact that you've just finished reading this book tells me that you were called to it for a reason (likely one only you understand), but if someone isn't ready to learn about these five steps, they will not hear you no matter how clearly you explain them, and that's perfectly okay! Continue showing up in your power. One day, when that person asks you how, why, or what you did to become so comfortable in your story, sit them down with a smile and pull out this book.

Notes

1. Brené Brown, *Dare to Lead: Brave Work. Touch Conversations. Whole Hearts.*, Random House, 2018, New York.

2. What Happened To You? Conversations on Trauma, Resilience, and Healing, 2021, Bruce D. Perry and Oprah Winfrey

3. Edward L. Deci and Richard M. Ryan, *Intrinsic Motivation and Self-Determination in Human Behavior* (New York, NY: Plenum, 1985).

4. Charles Duhigg, 'What Google Learned From Its Quest to Build the Perfect Team,' *New York Times Magazine*, February 28, 2016, URL: https://www.nytimes.com/2016/02/28/magazine/what-google-learned-from-its-quest-to-build-the-perfect-team.html

5. Eckhart Tolle, *A New Earth: Awakening to your life's purpose*, Penguin, 2008, New York.

Acknowledgements

This book wouldn't exist without my parents, Kerri and Sammy. Thank you for literally everything.

I'm a big believer that, much like people, books also have a way of finding you when you need them. When I happened to come across the Instagramable cover of *Make You Happen* by Jordanna Levin, I was unaware that she would play such an integral part in my journey. Having never navigated the world of publishing, I needed my own knowledgeable guide to get what was burning in my heart into a pitch for the right publisher, and Jordanna did beyond that. I'm immensely grateful to have had you in my corner, supporting me from day one. You have been a deep source of encouragement and guidance, and I'm so thankful you answered my email.

To my luminous publisher Natasha Gilmour, thank you for believing in this idea with all of your light. You gave me the space and trust required to bring this book to life, intuitively knowing I was the author to birth it whilst gently guiding me along the way. I am so proud to be a part of the kind press fold and honoured to be included among your range of authors. That said, I'd also like to thank the team at the kind press for your incredible support and work.

To my amazing editor Katie Bosher, I cannot thank you enough for seeing this project's merit and shepherding it to where it is today. Without your insights and brilliance, I'm not convinced it would shimmer the same. Thank you for helping me make it excellent.

A big shout out to Christa Moffitt for the incredible cover design and for convincing me (along with Natasha) that my good vibe energy came through my photo and that I needed to be on the cover.

To my beautiful friends and family who encouraged me to keep going when the days were long, and my brain felt heavy. Your flowers, notes and words were so appreciated.

To all the inspiring storytellers I named in the book, thank you for sharing a story with me that left a mark.

I'd also like to acknowledge the clients, readers, listeners and likers along the way. Without your openness to my story and message, this book wouldn't exist. This book is your book just as much as it is mine.

To all the storytellers and my guides who have gone before me, with infinite tenderness, thank you for lighting the path.

And finally, I'd like to end with my most enormous thanks to you, Ben. Your support and love on this journey have been profound.

About the Author

Janika Galloway is a highly sought-after guide, author and speaker empowering individuals to unlock their storytelling power and manifest the narratives they desire. Spending over a decade working internationally in high-level corporate public relations and marketing positions, Janika now guides others by merging her professional expertise with her personal gifts in a nurturing, warm and playful way.

In addition to her guiding role, Janika hosts the popular storytelling podcast Just You, which has gained recognition from Spotify as one of the top 17% most followed podcasts. Known for her gentle yet effective approach, Janika offers practical tips and actionable advice through her sessions, workshops, and content for storytellers that want to step into their power.

For more information, visit www.janikagalloway.com and connect with Janika on Instagram.